Pittsburgh Series in Bibliography

Supplement to

F. SCOTT FITZGERALD

Supplement to

F. Scott Fitzgerald

A DESCRIPTIVE BIBLIOGRAPHY

Matthew J. Bruccoli

UNIVERSITY OF
PITTSBURGH PRESS
1980

Published by the University of Pittsburgh Press, Pittsburgh, Pa. 15260
Copyright © 1980, University of Pittsburgh Press
All rights reserved
Feffer and Simons, Inc., London
Manufactured in the United States of America

Library of Congress Cataloging in Publication Data

Bruccoli, Matthew Joseph, 1931–
    Supplement to F. Scott Fitzgerald.

    (Pittsburgh series in bibliography)
    Includes index.
    1. Bruccoli, Matthew Joseph, 1931–   F. Scott
Fitzgerald 2. Fitzgerald, Francis Scott Key, 1896–
1940—Bibliography. I. Bruccoli, Matthew Joseph,
1931–   F. Scott Fitzgerald. II. Title
III. Series.
Z8301.2.B69 Suppl   [PS3511.I9]   016.813'5'2   79-21728
ISBN 0-8229-3409-4

Once Again
to
Scottie

Contents

Acknowledgments

ALL bibliographies are collaborations. My principal collaborators on this volume were Inge Kutt, Karen Rood, Susan Walker, Meredith Walker, Margaret Duggan, and Carol Johnston, who also prepared the index.

The interlibrary loan staff at the Cooper Library, University of South Carolina, always came through; and I am especially obligated to Joyce Werner, Harriet Oglesbee, and Michele Yarus. It is a pleasure to work at the United States Copyright Office. I received many courtesies from the staffs of the British Library and the Bodleian Library. Susan Manakul helped at the Library of Congress. My debts are enormous to the staff at the Special Collections Department at the Princeton University Library: Alexander Clark, Richard Ludwig, Agnes Sherman, Jean F. Preston, Mardel Pacheco, Margarethe Fitzell, Ann Farr, and Charles E. Green. Frederic E. Rusch found four of the English dust jackets that eluded me. Richard Taylor performed the photographic work with his usual cheerful competence. Anthony Rota of Bertram Rota Ltd. and Muriel Hamilton of Hampton Books were among the many dealers who found books for me. Charles Scribner III generously answered questions about the Scribners editions. C. E. Frazer Clark, Jr., is my partner in all projects. William Nolte and George Geckle, chairmen of the Department of English at the University of South Carolina while this bibliography was in progress, provided research assistance. Provost Keith Davis arranged a travel grant. Frederick A. Hetzel and Louise Craft of the University of Pittsburgh Press make this series possible.

The dedication page indicates my greatest debt.

Introduction

THIS *Supplement* corrects and updates my *F. Scott Fitzgerald: A Descriptive Bibliography* (1972). It also adds two new sections to the bibliography: J. Translations and K. Republications (of Fitzgerald's stories, poems, essays, and letters).

Sections A through I and Appendices 1, 2, 6, 7, 9, and 10 augment those parts of the *Bibliography*. Corrections and additions to entries in the *Bibliography* are keyed to the original entry and page numbers. New entries follow in their numerical order.

TERMS AND METHODS

Edition. All the copies of a book printed from a single setting of type—including all reprintings from standing type, from plates, or by photo-offset processes.

Printing. All the copies of a book printed at one time (without removing the type or plates from the press).

State. States occur only within single printings and are created by an alteration not affecting the conditions of publication or sale to *some* copies of a given printing (by stop-press correction or cancellation of leaves). There can be no first state without a second state.

Issue. Issues occur only within single printings and are created by an alteration affecting the conditions of publication or sale to *some* copies of a given printing (usually a title-page alteration). There can be no first issue without a second issue.

Edition, printing, state and *issue* have been restricted to the sheets of the book. Binding or dust-jacket variants have no bearing on these terms.[1] Binding variants in this bibliography are treated simply as binding variants; however, it can be assumed that the deposit copies at The Library of Congress and The British Library are early copies.

State and *issue* are the most abused terms in the vocabulary of bibliographical description. Many cataloguers use them interchangeably as well as ignorantly. Much would be gained for the profession of bibliography by the consistent and precise usage of these terms. *State* is easy to use correctly,

---

1. This statement holds for twentieth-century publishing. It is not possible to be so dogmatic for nineteenth-century publishing, when parts of a printing were marketed in different formats—e.g., cloth, paper, and two-in-one bindings. In such cases it is difficult to avoid calling the different bindings *issues* because they do represent a deliberate attempt to alter the condition of publication.

but *issue* is more troublesome. Some able bibliographers prefer to define issue in terms of publication or distribution, rather than of type pedigree. They argue that a new issue results whenever a complete printing is introduced into a publisher's series or whenever a complete printing is released by a new publisher or whenever sheets from a single printing are bound in cloth and paper. Nonetheless, *issue* has been treated conservatively in this volume.

The form of entry for first English editions or printings is somewhat condensed from the full form provided for American editions.

Dust jackets for Section A entries have been described in detail because they are part of the original publication effort and sometimes provide information about how the book was marketed. There is, of course, no certainty that a jacket now on a copy of a book was always on it.

For binding-cloth designations I have used the method proposed by Tanselle;[2] most of these cloth grains are illustrated in Jacob Blanck, ed., *The Bibliography of American Literature* (New Haven: Yale University Press, 1955–).

Color specifications are taken from the *ISCC–NBS Color Name Charts Illustrated with Centroid Colors* (National Bureau of Standards).[3] A color designation holds for subsequent lines unless a color change is stipulated.

The spines of bindings or dust jackets are printed horizontally unless otherwise stipulated.

In the descriptions of title pages, bindings, and dust jackets, the color of the lettering is always black, unless otherwise stipulated. The style of type is roman, unless otherwise stated.

The term *perfect binding* refers to books in which the pages are held together with adhesive along the back edge after the folds have been trimmed off—for example, most paperbacks.

Dates provided within brackets do not appear on the title page. Usually—but not invariably—they are taken from the copyright pages.

Cross-references to the *Supplement* are followed by double daggers (for example, "see F 89‡") to distinguish them from those referring to the original *Bibliography*.

Location symbols:

BL: British Library
Bodleian: Bodleian Library, Oxford University
LC: Library of Congress
Lilly: Lilly Library, Indiana University
MJB: Collection of Matthew J. Bruccoli
NjP: Princeton University Library
PSt: Pennsylvania State University Library

---

2. G. Thomas Tanselle, "The Specifications of Binding Cloth," *The Library*, 21 (September 1966), 246–247.

3. G. Thomas Tanselle, "A System of Color Identification for Bibliographical Description," *Studies in Bibliography*, 20 (1967), 203–234. The compiler feels that the use of the Centroid designations gives a false sense of precision. Oxidation and fading make precise color description difficult, if not impossible.

For paperbacks, the serial number provided is that of the first printing. Paperback publishers normally change the serial number in later printings, but this information has not been noted in this bibliography.

It is desirable in bibliographical description to avoid end-of-line hyphens in transcriptions. However, because of word lengths and a measured line, it sometimes is impossible to satisfy this requirement. End-of-line hyphens have been avoided wherever possible, and always where a hyphen would create ambiguity.

A bibliography is outdated the day it goes to the printer. Additions and corrections are earnestly solicited.

The University of South Carolina
21 August 1978

A. Separate Publications

A 3 THE EVIL EYE

Binding (p. 10): Some copies may have been bound in limp leather.

Note two: There is a commercial cassette recording of the songs from Fitzgerald's three Triangle Club shows performed by the After-Dinner Opera Company of New York: *F. Scott Fitzgerald: Triangle Club Songs* (Bloomfield Hills, Mich., & Columbia, S.C.: Bruccoli Clark, 1979).

A 5 THIS SIDE OF PARADISE

A 5.1.a

Dust jacket (p. 15): A jacket with '$1.75/NET' on the spine is in the collection of R. H. Gresh; priority undetermined.

Note one (p. 17): See James L. W. West III, "The Corrections Lists for F. Scott Fitzgerald's *This Side of Paradise*," *Studies in Bibliography*, XXVI (1973), 254–264.

176.36 Johnston [Johnson 7

Note two (p. 18): See James L. W. West III, "The Second Serials of *This Side of Paradise* and *The Beautiful and Damned*," *Papers of the Bibliographical Society of America*, LXXIII (First Quarter 1979), 63–74.

Note five: The Scribners file copy with corrections in an unknown hand is in the Bruccoli Collection.

A 5.1.c *(p. 19)*

Probably 500 copies of *TSOP* with tipped-in "Author's Apology." One specially bound copy has been seen at ViU. (PS 3511. 19. T45. 1920b. 709285): blue boards and orange cloth shelfback with printed paper label.

A 5.2.a

Dust jacket (p. 22): Front has the W. E. Hill drawing that appeared on the American dust jacket: '[white outlined in black] THIS SIDE OF | PARADISE | By F. Scott Fitzgerald | [orange] COLLINS' 'FIRST NOVEL' LIBRARY'. Spine: '[black] This Side | of | Paradise | F. SCOTT | FITZGERALD | [orange] 'FIRST NOVEL' | LIBRARY | [white price against black circle] | [black Collins seal] | [black] COLLINS'. Back: 'Collins' New Novels | SPRING, 1921 | [thin and thick rules] | [9 titles beginning with *Mainwaring* and ending with *Adam and Caroline*] | [leaf] | Collins' First Novel Library | SPRING TITLES | [4 titles beginning with *Kimono* and ending with *TSOP*] | [thick and thin rules] | W. Collins Sons & Co. Ltd. :: 48 Pall Mall, S.W. 1'. Front flap lists 3 novels by Francis Brett Young, 4 novels by J. D. Beresford, and 4 novels by Beresford in preparation; back flap has blurbs for the sixth impression of *Potterism* by Rose Macaulay.

3

THIS SIDE OF PARADISE

By F. Scott Fitzgerald

COLLINS FIRST NOVEL LIBRARY

1449
This Side of Paradise
F. SCOTT FITZGERALD
"FIRST NOVEL LIBRARY"
7/6 net
COLLINS

Dust jacket for A 5.2.a

Location: University Library, Cambridge (21 July 1921).

Note two: See Frederic E. Rusch, "Addenda to Bruccoli: Four Additional Fitzgerald Dust Jackets," *Fitzgerald/Hemingway Annual 1977,* pp. 13–18.

A5.2.c *(p. 23)*

This reprint has been located in the collection of Anthony M. Carr.

A5.3 *(p. 23)*

A 1950 second printing has been reported.

A5.4 *(p. 23)*
New York: Dell, [1954]. #D 140. Wrappers.

A5.9 *(p. 24)*

Includes "Spires and Gargoyles," "The Egoist Considers," and "Narcissus off Duty."

EXCERPTS FROM *TSOP*

A5.11
Modern Women in Love, ed. Christina Stead and William Blake. New York: Dryden Press, 1945. Excerpt, pp. 131–145.

A5.12
Approaches to Prose, ed. Caroline Shrodes and Justine Van Gundy. New York: Macmillan, [1959]. Excerpt, pp. 561–578.

A5.13
Fitzgerald and the Jazz Age, ed. Malcolm and Robert Cowley. New York: Scribners, [1966]. Excerpts, pp. 7–9, 41–46.

A6 FLAPPERS AND PHILOSOPHERS

A6.1.a

Note one (p. 28): Fitzgerald asked Maxwell Perkins to make the revision from 'panoply' to 'panorama' on 12 August 1920.

A6.2.a

Dust jacket (p. 31): Front has the W. E. Hill drawing that appeared on the American dust jacket: '[white outlined in black] FLAPPERS AND | PHILOSOPHERS | By F. Scott Fitzgerald | [orange] *Author of* "THIS SIDE OF PARADISE"'. Spine: '[orange] FLAPPERS | AND | PHILOS- | OPHERS | [greenish black] F. SCOTT | FITZGERALD | [white price against orange circle] | [greenish black Collins seal] | [greenish black] COLLINS'. Back: '[greenish black] Collins' New Novels | SPRING, 1922 | [thick and thin rules] | [13 titles beginning with *The Return* and ending with *Mainspring*] | [thin and thick rules] | W. COLLINS SONS & CO. LTD. :: 48 PALL MALL, S.W. 1'. Front flap has *F&P* blurb; back flap has *TSOP* blurb.

Dust jacket for A6.2.a

Location: University Library, Cambridge (4 April 1922).

Note: 80.25–6   white, of brown and yellow   [white, brown, and yellow

A6.3 *(p. 32)*

Reprinted in Scribner Library: New York: Scribners, [1972]. #SL371. On copyright page: 'A.8.72 (C)'. Wrappers.

A8 THE BEAUTIFUL AND DAMNED

A8.1.a

Dust jacket (p. 35):   Maxwell Perkins to Fitzgerald, 10 February 1922: "In the second twenty thousand, we are printing the lettering of the title in black and the disk is in quite a deep orange." Another copy with this variant jacket was sold at Swann Galleries on 4 May 1978 (Sale #1101).

Note one (p. 37):   The conclusion of the *Metropolitan* serial was omitted from the book by Fitzgerald.

Note two (p. 38):   See James L. W. West III, "The Second Serials of *This Side of Paradise* and *The Beautiful and Damned*," *Papers of the Bibliographical Society of America*, LXXIII (First Quarter 1979), 63–74.

Note three (p. 38):   In 1923 *B&D* was offered as a subscription premium by *Screenland*, VI (March 1923), p. 7.

A8.1.b₁ *(p. 40)*

| COPYRIGHT, 1921, 1922, BY THE METROPOLITAN PUBLICATIONS, INC. |

A8.1.d *(p. 41)*

Scribners sheets in A. L. Burt binding. Possibly sheets of the third printing.

A8.1.e *(p. 41)*
Fifth printing: New York: A. L. Burt, [1924].

A8.1.f *(p. 42)*

Pages renumbered and preliminary pages reset.

A8.1.j

New York: Scribners, [1977]. Hudson River Editions. On copyright page: '1 . . . 19 B/C 20 . . . 2'.

A8.2.a

Dust jacket (p. 44):   Back: 'Collins' New Novels | AUTUMN 1922 | [thick and thin rules] | [14 titles beginning with *Pilgrim's Rest* and ending with *The Deaves Affair*] | [thin and thick rules] | W. COLLINS SONS & CO. LTD. :: 48 PALL MALL, S.W. 1'. Back flap lists 6 novels by Francis Brett Young, 8 novels by J. D. Beresford, and 2 works by Walter de la Mare.

Location: University Library, Cambridge (9 November 1922).

Dust jacket for A.8.2.a

A 8.6
The American Treasury 1455–1955, ed. Clifton Fadiman and Charles Van Doren. New York: Harper, [1955]. Excerpt, p. 954.

A 8.7
The Classic Woman, ed. James Sterling Moran. [New York: Playboy Press, 1971]. Excerpts, pp. [12], [34], [64].

A 9 TALES OF THE JAZZ AGE

A 9.1.a

Note (p. 48): The revision at 232.6 was probably made in the third printing. Type batter at 22.13, 27.30, 166.35, 217.1, 224.1, 252.1 probably differentiates the first two printings.

A 9.2.a$_1$ *(formerly* A 9.2.a, *p. 52)*
First English edition, first printing, first state [1923]

Dust jacket (p. 53): Spine: '[red] TALES | OF THE | JAZZ | AGE | [black] F. SCOTT | FITZGERALD | AUTHOR OF | "THE BEAUTIFUL AND | DAMNED" *etc.* | [white price against red circle] | [black seal] | [black] COLLINS'. Back: 'Collins' New Fiction | SPRING, 1923 | [thick and thin rules] | [14 titles beginning with *Love's Pilgrim* and ending with *Henry Brocken*] | [thin and thick rules] | W. Collins Sons & Co. Ltd. :: 48 Pall Mall, S.W. 1'. Front flap has blurb for *TJA;* back flap has blurbs for the second impression of *B&D.*

Locations: Bodleian 25612 e 1805 (April 1923); MJB; University Library, Cambridge (6 April 1923).

Note: There are 191 variants between the Scribners first printing and the Collins first printing (first state), of which two are substantives:

    39.4   hump   [39.1   lump
    114.12 you're   [113.33   your

A 9.2.a$_2$
First English edition, first printing, second state [1923]

[A]^8 B^8 ($\pm$ B 6,8) C^8 ($\pm$ C 2) D–I^8 K–U^8 X^8

    16.2; 16.31; 20.23; 24.24:   Diana Manners   [Cynthia Manley

Locations: BL (28 MAR 23); MJB (review copy).

Note: Also reported in Times Book Club binding.

A 10 THE VEGETABLE

A 10.1.a

Dust jacket (p. 56): Back flap has blurbs on Fitzgerald by H. L. Mencken, Sinclair Lewis, and Sidney Howard; also blurbs for *F&P* and *TSOP.*

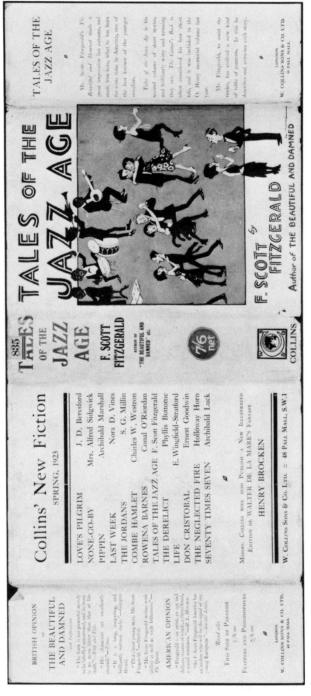

Dust jacket for A 9.2.a

A 10.1.c
Third printing (authorized): Clifton, N.J.: Augustus M. Kelley, 1972.

A 10.2
Second edition

THE VEGETABLE | or | from President to postman | By | F. SCOTT FITZGERALD | A new edition with unpub- | lished scenes and correc- | tions and an introduction | by Charles Scribner III | [8-line epigraph] | CHARLES SCRIBNER'S SONS   NEW YORK

1976. Published in cloth and wrappers (#SL644). On copyright page:

'1 . . . 19 C/C 20 . . . 2'
'1 . . . 19 C/P 20 . . . 2'.

A 10.3
Third edition

F. Scott Fitzgerald | THE VEGETABLE | *Edited with Notes* | *by* | SUSUMU KAWANISHI | MIKIO INUI | TSURUMI SHOTEN | TOKYO

1978. Wrappers.

A 11 THE GREAT GATSBY

A 11.1.a

Note four (p. 62):   The first page of the manuscript was facsimiled in *The Princeton University Library Chronicle,* XII (Summer 1951), following p. 182.

Note five: See Matthew J. Bruccoli, *Apparatus for F. Scott Fitzgerald's* The Great Gatsby *[Under the Red, White, and Blue]* (Columbia: University of South Carolina Press, [1974]). Also 50 numbered copies in facsimile of the 1925 binding.

Note six: See Andrew T. Crosland, *A Concordance to F. Scott Fitzgerald's* The Great Gatsby (Detroit: Bruccoli Clark | Gale Research, [1975]).

Note seven: Two pages of the first MS are facsimiled in *The Princeton University Library Chronicle,* XXXIX (Spring 1978). See F 89‡.

A 11.8 *(p. 67)*

| F. Scott Fitzgerald |

Reprinted 1970, 1971 (twice), 1972, 1973 (twice), 1974 (twice).

A 11.13 *(p. 68)*

Reprinted in wrappers and cloth. On copyright page of latest cloth printing:

'7 . . . 19 M/P 20 . . . 6'
'5 . . . 19 M/C 20 . . . 4'.

Also reprinted by Caves Books (Taipei, Formosa, 1976?).

A 11.25
Fifteenth American edition

THE GREAT GATSBY | BY | F. SCOTT FITZGERALD | [4-line epigraph] | —THOMAS

PARKE D'INVILLIERS | [around Bantam device] • BANTAM BOOKS • LONDON TO-RONTO NEW YORK

1974. #T7448. Wrappers. 12 printings, March–July 1974.

A 11.26
Sixteenth American edition

[on white within decorated single-rule frame surrounded by gray] [script] The | [roman] GREAT | GATSBY | [script] by | [roman] F. SCOTT FITZGERALD | A Limited Edition | [leaf] | THE FRANKLIN LIBRARY | Franklin Center, Pennsylvania | 1974

On p. v: 'This limited edition of | THE GREAT GATSBY | is published exclusively for | subscribers to | The Franklin Library | collection | The 100 Greatest Books of All Time'.

A 11.27
Seventeenth American edition

The Great Gatsby | BY | F. SCOTT FITZGERALD | [4-line epigraph] | —THOMAS PARKE D'INVILLIERS | *CHARLES SCRIBNER'S SONS* | *New York*

1975.

[i–vi] 1–121 [122].

On copyright page of latest printing:

'37 39 M/P 40 38 36'
'33 35 37 39 M/C 40 38 36 34 32'.

See Margaret M. Duggan, "Editorial," *Fitzgerald/Hemingway Annual 1976*, p. 303.

A 11.28
Sixth English edition

THE GREAT GATSBY | F. Scott Fitzgerald | [device] | LYTHWAY PRESS | BATH

1975. Large-print edition.

A 11.29
Seventh English edition

The | Great Gatsby | *and* | The | Last Tycoon | [rule] | SCOTT FITZGERALD | *with an Introduction* | *by* | J. B. PRIESTLEY | BOOK CLUB ASSOCIATES   LONDON

1977. Reprint from Bodley Head plates. See AA 5.

A 11.30
Eighteenth American edition

THE | SCRIBNER | QUARTO | OF MODERN | LITERATURE | Edited by | A. WALTON LITZ | CHARLES SCRIBNER'S SONS | NEW YORK

1978. Pp. 208–264.

EXCERPTS FROM GG

A 11.31
Taken at the Flood, ed. Ann Watkins. New York: Harper, 1946. Excerpt, pp. 32–43.

A 11.32
Better Reading, II: Literature, ed. Walter Blair and John Gerber. Chicago: Scott, Fores-man, 1948. Excerpt, pp. 172–176.

A 11.33
These Would I Choose, ed. Alec Waugh. London: Low, [1948]. Excerpts, pp. 74–76, 125–126.

A 11.34
Center, Stella S. *The Art of Book Reading.* New York: Scribners, 1952. Excerpt from *The Great Gatsby* rendered for speed-reading, pp. 272–274.

A 11.35
The American Treasury 1455–1955, ed. Clifton Fadiman and Charles Van Doren. New York: Harper, 1955. Excerpt, pp. 954–955.

A 11.36
An Anthology of American Humor, ed. Brom Weber. New York: Crowell, [1962]. Ex-cerpt, pp. 523–532.

A 11.37
Advanced Spanish Composition, ed. Cyril A. Janes and Alec Payne. London: Oxford University Press, 1971. Excerpt, pp. 93–94.

A 11.38
In the Presence of This Continent, ed. Robert Baylor and James Moore. New York: Holt, Rinehart & Winston, [1971]. Epigraph, p. i.

A 11.39
The Saturday Evening Post Automobile Book. Indianapolis: Curtis, [1977]. Excerpt, pp. 77–91.

A 14 TENDER IS THE NIGHT

A 14.1.a

Dust jacket (p. 79): A later jacket has blurbs by Mary Colum, Gilbert Seldes, and Marjorie Kinnan Rawlings on the front flap. Reported in *J. Stephan Lawrence . . . Cata-logue 38* (Winter 1977–78), #510.

Note two (p. 81): TITN was serialized in 4 installments of *Scribner's Magazine,* XCV (January–April 1934). The text was slightly bowdlerized.

Note three: TITN was a Literary Guild alternate in June 1934.

A 14.1.a† *(p. 81)*

Another copy was sold at Swann Galleries, 11 September 1975 (Sale #996); a third copy is in the Bruccoli Collection.

A 14.6 *(p. 85)*

Reprinted: New York: Scribners, [1977]. Hudson River Editions. On copyright page: '1 . . . 19 B/C 20 . . . 2'.

EXCERPTS FROM *TITN*

A 14.9
Reading Writing and Rewriting, ed. W. T. Moynihan et al. Philadelphia & New York: Lippincott, [1964]. Excerpt, p. 180.

A 14.10
Fitzgerald and the Jazz Age, ed. Malcolm and Robert Cowley. New York: Scribners, [1966]. Excerpt, pp. 36–38.

A 14.11
Cole, ed. Robert Kimball and Brendan Gill. New York, Chicago, & San Francisco: Holt, Rinehart & Winston, [1971]. Excerpt, p. 53.

A 14.12
The Novel, ed. Richard Freedman. New York: Newsweek Books, [1975]. Excerpt, pp. 176–177.

A 15 TENDER IS THE NIGHT
Revised edition

A 15.1.a

Note two (p. 88):   Appendix includes the "Wanda Breasted" episode and first publications of the "Monsieur Irv" episode. "Wanda Breasted" was previously published as "The World's Fair"; see C 308, B 40.

A 15.1.f *(p. 89)*

Scribners reports that the plates for the revised text were also inadvertently used for the "Q" printing.

A 15.3 *(p. 92)*

Reprinted 1971, 1972, 1973, 1974.

A 16 THE TRUE STORY OF APPOMATTOX *(p. 93)*

A third copy was sold at Sotheby Parke Bernet, 29 March 1977 (Sale #3966).

A 17 TAPS AT REVEILLE

A 17.1.a

Note (p. 98):   *TAR* was a Literary Guild alternate in June 1935.

A 17.2.c
New York: Scribners, [1976]. Hudson River Editions. On copyright page: '1 . . . 19C/C20 . . . 2'.

A 18 THE LAST TYCOON

A 18.1.a

Note two (p. 102): A typescript editorial apparatus for *LT* by Matthew J. Bruccoli has been deposited at the following libraries: Library of Congress, Princeton University, British Library, Caroliniana (University of South Carolina), and Lilly (Indiana University). See also Bruccoli, *"The Last of the Novelists" F. Scott Fitzgerald and* The Last Tycoon (Carbondale & Edwardsville: Southern Illinois University Press, 1977). See B 103‡.

A 18.1.b *(p. 102)*
Second printing: New York: Scribners, 1941. The copyright page omits the 'A' but retains the seal.

A 18.1.c
New York: Scribners, 1945.

A 18.1.d
New York: Scribners, 1947.

A 18.1.e
New York: Scribners, 1948.

A 18.1.f *(formerly* A 18.1.c, *p. 102)*
New York: Scribners, 1951. *LT* and *GG* only; omits stories. See A 11.2.b.

A 18.1.g *(formerly* A 18.1.d, *p. 102)*
Modern Standard Authors Three Novels of F. Scott Fitzgerald. New York: Scribners, [1953]. See AA 4.

A 18.1.h *(formerly* A 18.1.e, *p. 102)*
New York: Scribners, [1958]. *LT* only. On copyright page: 'A-4.58 [MH]'.

A 18.1.i *(formerly* A 18.1.f, *p. 102)*
New York: Scribners, [1959]. On copyright page: 'B-4.59 [MH]'.

A 18.1.j *(formerly* A 18.1.g, *p. 102)*
New York: Scribners, [1960]. On copyright page: 'C-6.60 [MH]'.

A 18.1.k *(formerly* A 18.1.h, *p. 103)*
New York: Scribners, [1963]. On copyright page: 'D-3.63 [MH]'.

A 18.1.l *(formerly* A 18.1.i, *p. 103)*
New York: Scribners, [1965]. On copyright page: 'E-3.65 [MH]'.

A 18.1.m *(formerly* A 18.1.j, *p. 103)*
New York: Scribners, [1970]. Scribner Library #SL242. On copyright page: 'A-9.70 [M]'. Wrappers.

A 18.1.n
Taipei, Formosa: Big Wave, [   ].

A 18.1.o
New York: Scribners, [1977]. Hudson River Editions. On copyright page: '1 . . . 19 B/C
20 . . . 2'.

A 18.3 *(p. 106)*
Reprinted 1971, 1972, 1974 (twice), 1977.

A 18.5
Third English edition

The | Great Gatsby | *and* | The | Last Tycoon | [rule] | SCOTT FITZGERALD | *with an
Introduction by* | J. B. PRIESTLEY | BOOK CLUB ASSOCIATES   LONDON

1977. Reprint from Bodley Head plates. See AA 5.

A 18.6
Third American edition

THE LAST | TYCOON | [thick and thin rules] | F. Scott Fitzgerald | Foreword by Edmund
Wilson | [around Bantam seal] • BANTAM BOOKS • LONDON NEW YORK TORONTO

1976. #10419-5. Wrappers.

EXCERPT FROM *LT*

A 18.7
In the Presence of This Continent, ed. Robert Baylor and James Moore. New York: Holt,
Rinehart & Winston, [1971]. Excerpt, pp. 200–203.

A 19 THE CRACK-UP

A 19.1.a

Contents (p. 109):   The transposition of the titles for "Handle With Care" and "Pasting
It Together" was corrected by the 11th paperbound printing.

A 19.1.b *(p. 111)*

The second printing (1945) of *The Crack-Up* was 3,560 copies; the third printing
(1945), 4,620; the fourth printing (1946), 5,341 copies.

A 19.1.c *(p. 111)*

Reprint noted: 'ELEVENTH PRINTING'.

A 19.2.a

Essays and stories (p. 113):   "Echoes of the Jazz Age," "My Lost City," "Ring," "The
Crack-Up," "Handle With Care," "Pasting It Together," "Early Success," "Gretchen's
Forty Winks," "The Last of the Belles," "Babylon Revisited," "A Patriotic Short," "Two
Old-Timers," "Financing Finnegan."

A 19.2.c *(p. 114)*

Reprinted 1974 (twice).

A 20 THE STORIES OF F. SCOTT FITZGERALD

A 20.1.l
New York: Scribners, [1979]. Edited by Malcolm Cowley. Hudson River Editions. On copyright page: '1 . . . 19 B/C 20 . . . 2'.

A 20.2
Second edition

THE BODLEY HEAD | SCOTT | FITZGERALD | *VOLUME 5* [6] | SHORT STORIES | SELECTED AND INTRODUCED BY | MALCOLM COWLEY | [device] | THE BODLEY HEAD | LONDON

1963. 2 volumes.

Adds 12 stories to 1951 Cowley selection. See AA 5‡.

A 20.3
Third edition

THE STORIES OF | F. Scott Fitzgerald | [decorated rule] | *A Selection of 28 Stories* | *With an Introduction by* | MALCOLM COWLEY | CHARLES SCRIBNER'S SONS *New York*

1972. Added to the 4-volume set distributed by the Literary Guild of America and its associated book clubs. See AA 15‡.

[A–B] [i–v] vi [vii] viii–xxix [xxx] [1–3] 4 [5] 6–541 [542–544]; first page of each story unnumbered.

A 20.4
Fourth edition

[within decorated brownish orange frame] [black] The Stories of | F. Scott Fitzgerald | A Selection with Notes by Malcolm Cowley | *Illustrated by John Collier* | [decoration] | [orange] A LIMITED EDITION | [black] THE FRANKLIN LIBRARY | Franklin Center, Pennsylvania | 1977

[i–xvi] [1–4] 5–585 [586–592]; editor's notes and illustrations unnumbered. Accompanied by pamphlet, *Notes from the Editors.*

On p. vi: *'This limited edition | is published by | The Franklin Library | exclusively for subscribers to* | THE COLLECTED STORIES OF | THE WORLD'S GREATEST WRITERS'.

A 22 AFTERNOON OF AN AUTHOR

A 22.1.b *(p. 123)*

Reprinted 5 times in cloth. See next entry.

A 22.1.c *(p. 123)*

Reprinted once in the Scribner Library. On copyright page of latest cloth printing:

'3 . . . 19 C/P 20 . . . 2'
'7 . . . 19 C/C 20 . . . 6'.

A 22.2

Review copy (p. 125):   Book sheets bound in very light greenish blue (#171) wrappers with white label on front printed in black: 'AFTERNOON | OF AN AUTHOR | A SELECTION OF UNCOLLECTED | STORIES AND ESSAYS WITH AN | INTRODUCTION AND NOTES BY | ARTHUR MIZENER | [tapered rule] | F. Scott Fitzgerald'. Location: MJB.

A 24 THE PAT HOBBY STORIES

A 24.2.b
Second English printing: [Harmondsworth]: Penguin, [1974].

A 26 THE LETTERS OF F. SCOTT FITZGERALD

A 26.1.a
Note two (p. 138):   Copies distributed by the Book-of-the-Month Club in 1974 can be identified by a blindstamped square on the back cover.

A 26.1.d *(formerly A 26.2, p. 139)*
First edition, first English printing: London: Bodley Head, [1964].

A 26.1.e *(formerly A 26.1.d, p. 138)*
[New York: Dell], 1965.

A 26.2 *(formerly A 26.3, p. 141)*
Second American edition: [New York: Dell, 1966].

A 26.3 *(formerly A 26.4, p. 141)*
First English edition: [Harmondsworth]: Penguin, [1968].

A 26.4 *(formerly A 26.5, p. 141)*
Third American edition: [New York: Bantam, 1971].

A 27 THE APPRENTICE FICTION OF F. SCOTT FITZGERALD

A 27.1.b
Second printing: New Brunswick: Rutgers University Press, [1974]. Wrappers.

A 28 THOUGHTBOOK OF FRANCIS SCOTT KEY FITZGERALD

Note (p. 147):   Printed from type of *The Princeton University Library Chronicle.* See C 316.

A 31 DEARLY BELOVED

Publication (p. 153):   No official publication date; the first copy was sold 24 February 1970.

A 32 F. SCOTT FITZGERALD IN HIS OWN TIME

A 32.1.b
Second printing: New York: Popular Library, [1974]. #445-08274-175. Wrappers.

A 33 DEAR SCOTT/DEAR MAX

A 33.1.b
First edition, first English printing [1973]

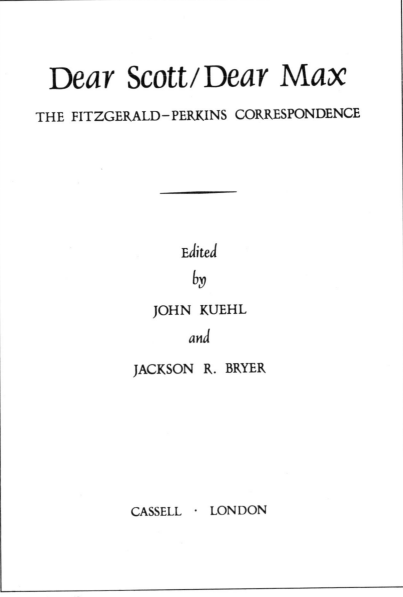

Dear Scott/ Dear Max

THE FITZGERALD–PERKINS CORRESPONDENCE

———

Edited

by

JOHN KUEHL

and

JACKSON R. BRYER

CASSELL · LONDON

A 33.1.b: 9⅛″ x 5¹⁵⁄₁₆″

CASSELL & COMPANY LTD.

35 Red Lion Square, London WC1R 4SG
Sydney, Auckland
Toronto, Johannesburg

Copyright © 1971 Charles Scribner's Sons

Some of the letters appeared first in Esquire Magazine.
Copyright © 1971 Charles Scribner's Sons.

Others letters are reprinted from the following books:
EDITOR TO AUTHOR: THE LETTERS OF
MAXWELL E. PERKINS,
edited by John Hall Wheelock.
Copyright © 1950 Charles Scribner's Sons.

THE LETTERS OF F. SCOTT FITZGERALD,
edited by Andrew Turnbull.
Copyright © 1963 Frances Scott Fitzgerald Lanahan.

All rights reserved. No part of this publication may be reproduced,
stored in a retrieval system, or transmitted, in any form or by any means,
electronic, mechanical, photocopying, recording or otherwise, without
the prior permission of Cassell and Company Ltd

First published in Great Britain 1973

ISBN 0 304 29150 1

PRINTED IN GREAT BRITAIN BY A. WHEATON & CO., EXETER

F 1272

Same pagination as Scribners printing.

[A]^8 B–I^8 K–S^8

Contents: Same as Scribners printing.

Typography and paper: Same as Scribners printing.

Binding: Strong purple (#218) V cloth (smooth). Spine: '[vertically] [white] Dear Scott [light blue (#181)] Dear Max | [horizontally, white] CASSELL'. White endpapers. All edges trimmed.

Dust jacket: Front and spine printed on coated deep blue (#179). Front: '[black scrollwork extending to spine] [white] Dear Scott | Dear Max | The Fitzgerald~Perkins | Correspondence | [black] Edited by John Kuehl | and Jackson Bryer'. Spine: '[vertically, white] Dear Scott Dear Max | [horizontally, black] CASSELL'. Back: '[within blue double-rules frame] [in black on white] ALSO PUBLISHED BY CASSELL | The Letters of | Aubrey Beardsley'. Front flap has blurb for *Scott | Max;* back flap: 'THE EDITORS'.

Publication: 3,000 copies. Published 22 March 1973. £3.50.

Printing: Printed and bound by A. Wheaton & Co., Exeter, Devon.

Locations: BL (26 APR 73); MJB (dj).

A 33.1.c
Third printing: New York: Scribners, [1973]. Scribner Library #SL460. On copyright page: '1 . . . 19 C/P 20 . . . 2'. Wrappers.

The letters of F Scott Fitzgerald and Maxwell E. Perkins record the relationship between a great writer and an incomparable editor. From 1919 to 1940, the correspondence reveals the genesis of a talent and the progress of a career. It shows the crucial importance of Perkins' perceptive counsel and steadying hand.

Dear Scott/Dear Max also illuminates an era. Both Fitzgerald and Perkins were eager to find new talent and support it; and they enjoyed anecdotes about the writers they knew. The letters are filled with acute remarks and fascinating details about Ernest Hemingway, Thomas Wolfe, Ring Lardner, Edmund Wilson, Willa Cather, Edith Wharton, Carl Van Vechten, and many more. The book is an important chapter in modern literary history.

First of all, however, *Dear Scott/Dear Max* is the record of a friendship between two men with very different natures who gave each other respect and loyalty.

£8.50 net

Dear Scott ᛞ Dear Max

The Fitzgerald-Perkins Correspondence

Edited by John Kuehl and Jackson Bryer

CASSELL

Dear Scott ᛞ Dear Max

CASSELL

THE EDITORS

JOHN KUEHL is Associate Professor of English at New York University where he teaches contemporary American literature and creative writing. A graduate of the University of Iowa, he took his Ph.D. at Columbia. He is the author of a number of studies in modern fiction and is currently at work on a book examining the work of John Hawkes.

JACKSON BRYER is Associate Professor of English at the University of Maryland. A graduate of Amherst, with a Ph.D. from the University of Wisconsin, he has written bibliographical and critical studies of Fitzgerald, Wallace Stevens, and other twentieth century writers.

ALSO PUBLISHED BY CASSELL

The Letters of
Aubrey Beardsley

EDITED BY

H. MAAS, J. L. DUNCAN and W. G. GOOD

"The most comprehensive edition published so far, and the book's a triumph. Here Beardsley comes alive as he has never come alive in any written work before . . . . Admirably edited."
—HAROLD KUEHL, *Sunday Telegraph*

"An imperative work of reference for further Beardsley studies; at the same time it brings our very close to an attractive and admirable personality."
—KAY WEAVERMAN, *Arts Review*

"This present volume is of great interest, revealing more of the artist himself and the people who surrounded him, at the same time providing a dramatic, amusing and in the end appallingly harrowing story."
—ANTHONY POWELL, *Daily Telegraph*

"An essential work for anyone who is interested in that fascinating and appalling period."
—PHILIP TOYNBEE, *Observer*

"The editing is both painstaking and tactfully helpful."
—DAVID PRYCE, *Guardian*

"The letters are fully and beautifully presented."
—MICHAEL FOOT, *London Evening Standard*

Jacket design: Keith Pointon
ISBN 0 304 29730 1

A 34 AS EVER, SCOTT FITZ—

A 34.1.a (*formerly* A 34)

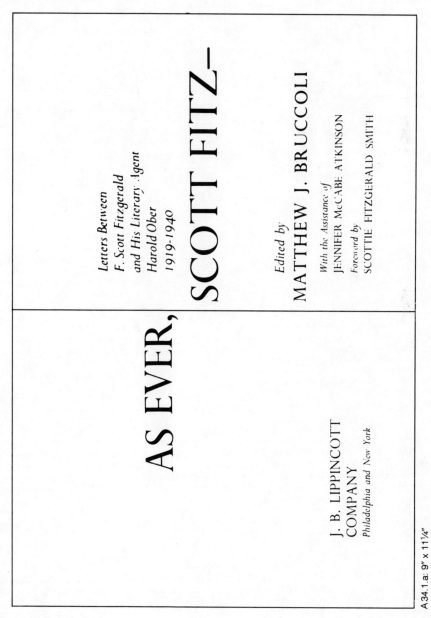

Letters Between
F. Scott Fitzgerald
and His Literary Agent
Harold Ober
1919–1940

AS EVER, SCOTT FITZ—

Edited by
MATTHEW J. BRUCCOLI

With the Assistance of
JENNIFER McCABE ATKINSON
Foreword by
SCOTTIE FITZGERALD SMITH

J. B. LIPPINCOTT
COMPANY
Philadelphia and New York

A 34.1.a: 9" x 11¼"

Original title-page illustration *(p. 162)* was made from an uncorrected proof. The correct reading in the fourth line on the right-hand page is '*Harold Ober*'.

Location (p. 164):   LC (16 MAY 1972).

A 34.1.b
First edition, first English printing (1973)

Letters Between
F. Scott Fitzgerald
and His Literary Agent
Harold Ober
1919-1940

AS EVER, SCOTT FITZ—

Edited by
MATTHEW J. BRUCCOLI

With the Assistance of
JENNIFER McCABE ATKINSON
Foreword by
SCOTTIE FITZGERALD SMITH

THE WOBURN PRESS
LONDON 1973

A 34.1.b: 9¹/₁₆″ x 11¾″

First published 1973 in Great Britain by
WOBURN BOOKS LIMITED
67 Great Russell Street, London WC1B 3BT

ISBN 0 7130 0098 8

Letters from F. Scott Fitzgerald which have been
published in *The Letters of F. Scott Fitzgerald*, edited
by Andrew Turnbull (copyright © 1963 by Frances
Scott Fitzgerald Lanahan), are reprinted with the
permission of Charles Scribner's Sons.

Copyright © 1972 by
S. J. Lanahan, Trustee; Anne Reid Ober; and Matthew J. Bruccoli

*Printed in Great Britain
by Unwin Brothers Limited,
The Gresham Press, Old Woking, Surrey, England*

Same pagination as Lippincott printing.

[1–29]⁸

Contents: Same as Lippincott printing.

Typography and paper: Same as Lippincott printing.

Binding: Deep purple blue (#197) V cloth (smooth). Spine goldstamped: 'Bruccoli |
and | Atkinson | [vertically, script] As Ever, Scott—Fitz | [horizontally] [Woburn device]
[roman] WOBURN | PRESS'. White endpapers with facsimiles of correspondence. All
edges trimmed.

Dust jacket: Light gray (#264) coated paper. Front: '[deep purple blue (#197) script]
As Ever, | Scott–Fitz | [sepia photo of Scott and Zelda Fitzgerald] | [black] Letters
Between F. Scott Fitzgerald | and His Literary Agent, Harold Ober | 1919–1940 | Edited
by Matthew J. Bruccoli'. Spine: 'Bruccoli | and | Atkinson | [vertically, deep purple blue
script] As Ever, Scott–Fitz | [horizontally, black] [Woburn device] | WOBURN | PRESS'.
Back has photos of Fitzgerald and Ober. Front and back flaps have blurbs for *AESF*
with note on editors.

Publication: 2,000 copies. Published 8 November 1973. £4.25.

Printing: Printed by Unwin Brothers Ltd., The Gresham Press, Old Woking, Surrey.

Locations: BL (28 NOV 74); MJB (dj).

Dust jacket for A34.1.b

A 35 THREE HOURS BETWEEN PLANES
First edition, first printing (1970)

Three Hours Between Planes F. SCOTT FITZGERALD

It was a wild chance but Donald was in the mood. healthy and bored, with a sense of tiresome duty done. He was now rewarding himself. Maybe.

When the plane landed he stepped out into a midwestern summer night and headed for the isolated pueblo airport. conventionalized as an old red "railway depot". He did not know whether she was alive, or living in this town, or what was her present name. With mounting excitement he looked through the phone book for her father who might be dead too, somewhere in these twenty years.

No. Judge Harmon Holmes Hillside 3194.

A woman's amused voice answered his inquiry for Miss Nancy Holmes.

"Nancy is Mrs. Walter Gifford now. Who is this?"

But Donald hung up without answering. He had found out what he wanted to know and had only three hours. He did not remember any Walter Gifford and there was another suspended moment while he scanned the phone book. She might have married out of town.

No. Walter Gifford Hillside 1191. Blood flowed back into his fingertips.

"Hello?"

"Hello. Is Mrs. Gifford there this is an old friend of hers."

"This is Mrs. Gifford."

He remembered, or thought he remembered. the funny magic in the voice.

"This is Donald Plant. I haven't seen you since I was twelve years old."

"Oh-h-h!" The note was utterly surprised. very polite, but he could distinguish in it neither joy nor certain recognition.

"—*Donald!*" added the voice. This time there was something more in it than struggling memory.

". . .when did you come back to town?" Then cordially, "Where *are* you?"

"I'm out at the airport for just a few hours."

"Well. come up and see me."

"Sure you're not just going to bed."

"Heavens, no!" she exclaimed. "I was sitting here having a highball by myself. Just tell your taxi man. . ."

On his way Donald analyzed the conversation. His words "at the airport" established that he had retained his position in the upper bourgeoisie. Nancy's aloneness might indicate that she had matured into an unattractive woman without friends. Her husband might be either away or in bed. And because she was always ten years old in his dreams the highball shocked him. But he adjusted himself with a smile she was very close to thirty.

At the end of a curved drive he saw a dark-haired little beauty standing against the lighted door, a glass in her hand. Startled by her final materialization, Donald got out of the cab, saying:

"Mrs. Gifford?"

She turned on the porch light and stared at him. wide-eyed and tentative. A smile broke through the puzzled expression.

"Donald it *is* you we all change so. Oh, this is re*mark*able!"

As they walked inside. their voices jingled the words "all these years." and Donald felt a sinking in his stomach. This derived in part from a vision of their last meeting when she rode past him on a bicycle, cutting him dead and in part from fear lest they have nothing to say. It was like a college reunion but there the failure to find the past was disguised by the hurried boisterous occasion. Aghast, he realized that this might be a long and empty hour. He plunged in desperately.

"You always were a lovely person. But I'm a little shocked to find you as beautiful as you are."

It worked. The immediate recognition of their changed state, the bold compliment, made them interesting strangers instead of fumbling childhood friends.

"Have a highball?" she asked. "No? Please don't think I've become a secret drinker, but this was a blue night. I expected my husband but he wired he'd be two days longer. He's very nice, Donald, and very attractive. Rather your type and coloring." She hesitated, " and I think he's interested in someone in New York and I don't know."

"After seeing you it sounds impossible," he assured her. "I was married for six years, and

A Book Society SEARCHLIGHT 116

Editors: Brian Meeson and Cliften Whiten

A 35: 11" x 8½"

Three Hours Between Planes F. SCOTT FITZGERALD | [text] | [within shield: BOOK | SOCI-ETY | SELECT | YOUR | OWN] A Book Society SEARCHLIGHT 116 | Editors: Brian Meeson and Cliften Whiten

On p. 4: '© THE BOOK SOCIETY OF CANADA LIMITED, 1970'.

Head title. Agincourt: Book Society of Canada, 1970.

Folio punched for loose-leaf binding: [1]^2; [1] 2–3 [4]

Contents: pp. 1–3: text; p. 4: teaching material. Accompanied by a single-leaf *COMMENTARY*.

Location: MJB.

A 36 THE BASIL AND JOSEPHINE STORIES

A 36.1.a
First edition, first printing [1973]

The Basil and Josephine Stories

by F. Scott Fitzgerald

Edited with an introduction by
JACKSON R. BRYER *and* JOHN KUEHL

A 36.1.a: 8^{15}⁄₁₆″ x 5^{15}⁄₁₆″

[i–vi] vii–xxix [xxx–xxxii] 1–287 [288]

[1–10]^{16}

Contents: p. i: half title; p. ii: *'BY F. SCOTT FITZGERALD';* p. iii: title; p. iv: copyright; pp. v–vi: *'Contents';* pp. vii–xxvi: *'Introduction';* pp. xxvii–xxix: *'Textual Note and Acknowledgments';* p. xxx: blank; p. xxxi: half title; p. xxxii: blank; pp. 1–287: text, headed *'I. Basil';* p. 288: blank.

14 stories: "That Kind of Party,"* "The Scandal Detectives," "A Night at the Fair," "The Freshest Boy," "He Thinks He's Wonderful," "The Captured Shadow," "The Perfect Life," "Forging Ahead," "Basil and Cleopatra," "First Blood," "A Nice Quiet Place," "A Woman with a Past," "A Snobbish Story,"* "Emotional Bankruptcy."* Asterisks follow previously uncollected stories.

Typography and paper: 6^{15}⁄₁₆″ (7⅝″) x 4⅝₁₆″ ; 40 lines per page. Running heads: rectos, story titles; versos, *'The Basil and Josephine Stories'.* Wove paper.

Binding: Dark purple red (#259) V cloth (smooth). Front blindstamped with silhouette of boy and girl standing on ornate decoration. Spine goldstamped: '[vertically] Kuehl [slash] Bryer | F. Scott Fitzgerald | THE BASIL AND | JOSEPHINE STORIES | Scribners'. Pale orange yellow (#73) endpapers. All edges trimmed. Brown and white bands at top and bottom.

Dust jacket: Printed on gray yellow (#90). Front: '[deep brown (#56)] F. Scott Fitzgerald | [dark red purple (#242) silhouette of boy and girl standing on ornate decoration] | [deep brown] THE BASIL | AND JOSEPHINE | STORIES | [dark red purple] EDITED BY | John Kuehl and Jackson Bryer'. Spine: '[vertically] [deep brown] F. Scott Fitzgerald THE BASIL AND | JOSEPHINE STORIES | [horizontally][dark red purple] Kuehl [slash] Bryer | [deep brown] Scribners'. Back: '[dark red purple silhouette of boy and girl standing on ornate decoration] | [deep brown][lamp device] | *Published by Charles Scribner's Sons • New York* | SBN 684-13398-9'. Front flap has blurb for *B&J;* back flap: 'The Editors'.

Publication: 10,000 copies. Published 23 August 1973. $8.95.

Printing: Printed and bound by Haddon Craftsmen, Scranton, Pa.

Locations: LC (SEP–5 1973); Lilly; MJB (dj).

Note: B&J was also distributed by The Reader's Subscription.

Review copy: Xeroxed galleys bound in very light blue green (#162) wrappers with very light green blue (#171) tape shelfback. White label on front printed in black: *'The Basil and Josephine Stories* | [double underline] | *by F. Scott Fitzgerald* | *Edited with an introduction* | *by* JACKSON R. BRYER *and* JOHN | KUEHL'. Location: MJB.

Dust jacket for A36.1.a

A 36.1.b
Second printing: [New York: Scribners, 1976]. Scribner Library #SL 661. On copyright page of paperbound printing:

'1 . . . 19 C/C 20 . . . 2'
'1 . . . 19 C/P 20 . . . 2'.

A 36.2
Second edition

F. SCOTT | FITZGERALD | THE BASIL AND | JOSEPHINE STORIES | Edited with an introduction by | Jackson R. Bryer and John Kuehl | POPULAR LIBRARY • NEW YORK

1976. #445-08506-175. Wrappers.

A 37 LEDGER (FACSIMILE)
First edition, only printing [1973]

F. Scott Fitzgerald's

LEDGER

A FACSIMILE

Introduction by Matthew J. Bruccoli

A Bruccoli Clark Book

NCR / MICROCARD EDITIONS
Washington, D.C.

A 37: 14¹¹/₁₆″ x 9⁷/₁₆″

104 pp.: [i–x] 1–17 50–55 (56–57) (58–59) 60 (61–63) 64–68 (69–73) 74–77 (100–102) 103–105 142–143 (144–150) 151–189 [190–200]; page numbers in parentheses indicate that Fitzgerald added numbers to the printed paginations.

[1–5]⁸ [6]⁴ 7⁸

Contents: p. i: half title; p. ii: blank; p. iii: title; p. iv: copyright and certificate of limitation; pp. v–vi: 'INTRODUCTION' by Matthew J. Bruccoli; p. vii: *'Textual Note:';* p. viii: 'Standard Blank Book *No.* 9'; p. ix: blank; p. x: 'Property of | F Scott Fitzgerald'; p. 1: 'Contents'; pp. 2–17: 'Record of Published Fiction–Novels, Plays, Stories'; p. 50: blank; pp. 51–77: 'Money Earned by Writing since Leaving Army'; pp. (100–102): blank; pp. 103–105: 'Published Miscelani (including movies) for which I was Paid'; p. 142: blank; p. 143: 'Zelda's Earnings'; pp. (144–150): blank; pp. 151–189: 'Outline Chart of my Life'; p. 190: blank; pp. 191–197: 'Appendix'; pp. 198–200: blank.

Typography and paper: Facsimile of holograph ledger. Wove paper.

Binding: Deep red (#13) coated CM (patterned sand grain) cloth, with black coated CM cloth shelfback. Greek key rule goldstamped vertically on front and back. Spine goldstamped: '[vertically] F. Scott Fitzgerald's LEDGER NCR'. Light olive gray (#112) endpapers with manufacturer's white label printed in black on front pastedown endpaper. All edges trimmed. Slipcase: Coated black paper with CM pattern.

Publication: 1,000 numbered copies. Published 1 September 1973. $40.

Printing: Printed by LithoCrafters, Ann Arbor, Mich. Bound by Tapley-Rutter, Moonachie, N.J.

Locations: LC (Nov 6–1975); Lilly; MJB; NjP; PSt.

Note one: Approximately 500 sets of sheets in the first printing were spoiled by the printer, and these sheets were reprinted. Therefore the "first printing" of *Ledger* includes sheets from 2 printings, which cannot be differentiated.

Note two: Promotional brochure for *Ledger* facsimiles 6 pages. [Washington: Bruccoli Clark/Microcard, 1973].

A 38 THE GREAT GATSBY (FACSIMILE)
First edition, only printing (1973)

F. Scott Fitzgerald

THE GREAT GATSBY

A Facsimile of the Manuscript

Edited with an Introduction by
Matthew J. Bruccoli
University of South Carolina

A Bruccoli Clark Book   Microcard Editions Books
Washington, D.C.
1973

A 38: 11¼" x 7¹¹⁄₁₆"

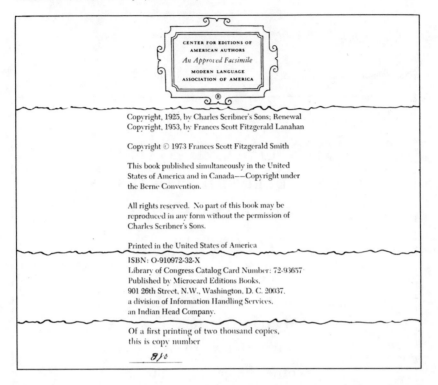

[i–vi] vii [viii] ix–xxxv [xxxvi–xxxviii] 1–302 [303–304] 305–308 [309–310] 311 [312] 313 [314] 315 [316] 317–336 [337–338]

[1–22]⁸ [23]⁴ [24]⁸

Contents: p. i: half title; p. ii: blank; p. iii: title; p. iv: copyright and certificate of limitation; p. v: *'To Fredson Bowers'*; p. vi: blank; p. vii: 'Contents'; p. viii: blank; pp. ix–x: 'Foreword' signed 'M.J.B.'; pp. xi–xii: 'Chronology'; pp. xiii–xxxv: 'Introduction' by Matthew J. Bruccoli; p. xxxvi: blank; p. xxxvii: 'Facsimile of the Manuscript'; p. xxxviii: blank; pp. 1–302: facsimile; p. 303: 'Specimen Galleys'; p. 304: blank; pp. 305–308: facsimiles of galleys; p. 309: 'Appendixes'; p. 310: blank; p. 311: 'Appendix 1'; p. 312: blank; p. 313: 'Appendix 2'; p. 314: blank; p. 315: 'Appendix 3'; p. 316: blank; pp. 317–336: 'Appendix 4'; p. 337: blank; p. 338: 'A Note on the Facsimile Process'.

Paper: Wove paper.

Binding: Black buckram, silverstamped. Front: 'THE GREAT GATSBY | *A Facsimile of the Manuscript*'. Spine: '[vertically] THE GREAT GATSBY'. Yellow gray (#93) endpapers. All edges trimmed. White bands at top and bottom. White V cloth slipcase.

Publication: 2,000 numbered copies. Published 1 November 1973. $50.

Printing: Printed by Meriden Gravure, Meriden, Conn. Bound by Complete Books, Philadelphia, Pa.

Locations: LC (NOV 6–1975); Lilly; MJB; NjP; PSt.

Note: Promotional brochure for *GG* manuscript facsimiles 2 pages. [Washington: Bruccoli Clark/Microcard, 1973].

A 39 BITS OF PARADISE

A 39.1.a
First edition, first printing [1973]

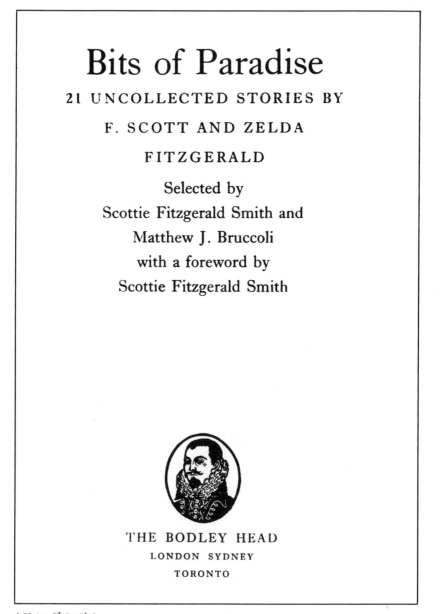

Bits of Paradise

21 UNCOLLECTED STORIES BY

F. SCOTT AND ZELDA

FITZGERALD

Selected by
Scottie Fitzgerald Smith and
Matthew J. Bruccoli
with a foreword by
Scottie Fitzgerald Smith

THE BODLEY HEAD
LONDON SYDNEY
TORONTO

A 39.1.a: 7⅞″ x 5½″

[i–vi] 1–385 [386]; 4 leaves of glossy photos inserted between pp. 210 and 211.

[1–23]⁸ [24]⁴ [25]⁸

Contents: p. i: half title; p. ii: blank; p. iii: title; p. iv: copyright; pp. v–vi: 'CONTENTS';
pp. 1–7: 'FOREWORD' by Scottie Fitzgerald Smith; pp. 8–13: 'PREFACE' by Matthew
J. Bruccoli; pp. 14–386: text, headed 'SCOTT'.

21 stories: "The Popular Girl" (FSF), "Love in the Night" (FSF), "Our Own Movie
Queen" (FSF & ZF), "A Penny Spent" (FSF), "The Dance" (FSF), "Jacob's Ladder"
(FSF), "The Swimmers" (FSF), "The Original Follies Girl" (ZF), "The Southern Girl" (ZF),
"The Girl the Prince Liked" (ZF), "The Girl with Talent" (ZF), "A Millionaire's Girl" (ZF),
"Poor Working Girl" (ZF), "The Hotel Child" (FSF), "A New Leaf" (FSF), "Miss Ella" (ZF),
"The Continental Angle" (ZF), "A Couple of Nuts" (ZF), "What a Handsome Pair!"
(FSF), "Last Kiss" (FSF), "Dearly Beloved" (FSF). First book publication for all except
"The Dance," "A Millionaire's Girl," "A New Leaf," "Last Kiss," and "Dearly Beloved."

Typography and paper: 5¹⁵⁄₁₆″ (6¼″) × 3⅝ ″; 36 lines per page. Wove paper.

Binding: Brilliant blue (#177) paper-covered boards with V pattern. Spine gold-
stamped: 'BITS OF | PARADISE | [star] | SCOTT | AND | ZELDA | FITZGERALD |

BODLEY | HEAD'. White wove endpapers. All edges trimmed; top edge stained light blue (#181).

Dust jacket: Printed on deep orange (#51). Front: '[within single-rule black frame] [brilliant yellow (#83)] F. Scott & | Zelda | Fitzgerald | [white] BITS OF | PARADISE | [brilliant green blue (#168) outlined in black] 21 New Stories'. Spine: '[deep orange rectangle within white frame] [vertically] [brilliant green blue] F. SCOTT & ZELDA FITZGERALD | [brilliant yellow] Bits of Paradise | [horizontally, black on white frame] BODLEY HEAD'. Back: solid deep orange. Front flap has blurb for *BOP;* back flap has ad for Bodley Head Scott Fitzgerald.

Publication: 5,000 copies. Published 29 November 1973. £3.50.

Printing: Printed and bound by William Clowes and Sons, Beccles, Suffolk.

Locations: BL (23 NOV 73); Lilly; MJB (dj).

Note: See Linda P. Berry, "The Text of *Bits of Paradise*," *Fitzgerald/Hemingway Annual 1975*, pp. 141–145.

Review copy: Page proofs bound in light yellow (#86) wrappers printed in black. Front: 'BODLEY HEAD | [head of Sir Thomas Bodley] | *UNCORRECTED PROOF COPY* | Bits of Paradise | 21 Uncollected Stories | F. SCOTT & ZELDA | FITZGERALD'. Spine: '[vertically] F. SCOTT AND ZELDA FITZGERALD Bits of Paradise'. In book dust jacket. Location: MJB.

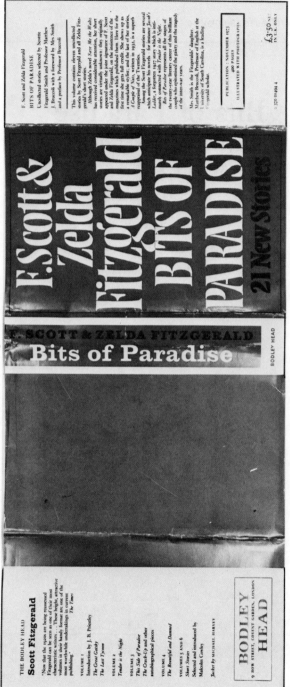

F. Scott and Zelda Fitzgerald

BITS OF PARADISE

Uncollected stories selected by Scottie Fitzgerald Smith and Professor Matthew J Bruccoli with a foreword by Mrs. Smith and a preface by Professor Bruccoli

This volume contains eleven uncollected stories by Scott Fitzgerald and all Zelda Fitzgerald's short stories.

Although Zelda's novel *Save Me the Waltz* has received considerable attention, her short stories are virtually unknown; they originally appeared under the joint signature of F. Scott and Zelda Fitzgerald, on the insistence of the magazines which published them. Here for the first time she gets full credit. She shows up as a remarkable stylist, and the last of her stories, *A Couple of Nuts*, written in 1932, is a superb reappraisal of the Twenties.

Among the Scott Fitzgerald stories are several which anticipate his novels - for instance *Jacob's Ladder*, a forgotten 1927 story which is intimately connected with *Tender is the Night*. *Bits of Paradise* represents all the stages of the twenty-year literary career of this brilliant couple who epitomised the gaiety and the tragedy of the inter-war years.

Mrs. Smith is the Fitzgeralds' daughter. Matthew Bruccoli, Professor of English at the University of South Carolina, is a leading Fitzgerald scholar.

PUBLICATION : NOVEMBER 1973
400 PAGES
ILLUSTRATED WITH PHOTOGRAPHS

£3·50 NET
IN U.K. ONLY

0 370 01494 4

F. Scott & Zelda Fitzgerald
BITS OF PARADISE
21 New Stories

F. SCOTT & ZELDA FITZGERALD
Bits of Paradise
BODLEY HEAD

THE BODLEY HEAD

Scott Fitzgerald

'Now that the 1920s are being reassessed Fitzgerald can be seen as one of their most characteristic writers...These bright, attractive volumes in their handy format are one of the most worthwhile undertakings in current publishing' *The Times*

VOLUME 1
Introduction by J. B. Priestley
The Great Gatsby
The Last Tycoon

VOLUME 2
Tender is the Night

VOLUME 3
The Side of Paradise
The Crack-Up and other autobiographical pieces

VOLUME 4
The Beautiful and Damned

VOLUMES 5 AND 6
Short Stories
Selected and introduced by Malcolm Cowley

Jacket by MICHAEL HARVEY

BODLEY HEAD
9 BOW STREET, COVENT GARDEN, LONDON

Dust jacket for A39.1.a

A 39.1.b
First edition, first American printing [1974]

Bits of Paradise

21 UNCOLLECTED STORIES BY

F. SCOTT AND ZELDA

FITZGERALD

Selected by
Matthew J. Bruccoli
with the assistance of
Scottie Fitzgerald Smith

Charles Scribner's Sons
New York

A 39.1.b: 8″ x 5⁷⁄₁₆″

[i–viii] 1–385 [386–392]

[1–6]¹⁶ [7]⁸ [8–13]¹⁶

Contents: p. i: half title; p. ii: blank; p. iii: title; p. iv: copyright; p. v: 'To Wanda Randall'; p. vi: blank; pp. vii–viii: 'CONTENTS'; pp. 1–7: 'FOREWORD' by Scottie Fitzgerald Smith; pp. 8–13: 'PREFACE' by Matthew J. Bruccoli; pp. 14–386: text; pp. 387–392: blank.

21 stories: Same as Bodley Head printing.

Typography and paper: Same as Bodley Head printing.

Binding: Black V cloth. Spine stamped in white: '[vertically] F. SCOTT AND ZELDA | FITZGERALD Bits of Paradise SCRIBNERS'. Dark red orange (#38) endpapers. All edges trimmed. Black and white bands at top and bottom.

Dust jacket: Printed on white. Front: '[black] F. Scott & | Zelda | Fitzgerald | [photo of Fitzgeralds with Renault] | [deep red orange (#36) script] Bits of Paradise | [black roman] 21 Uncollected Stories'. Spine: '[vertically, black] F. Scott & Zelda Fitzgerald | [horizontally, deep red orange] BITS OF | PARADISE | [black] SCRIBNERS'. Back: 3 photos of Fitzgeralds. Front and back flaps have blurb for *BOP.*

Publication: 6,000 copies. Published 26 September 1974. $7.95.

Printing: Printed and bound by Colonial Press, Clinton, Mass.

Locations: LC (OCT 15 1974); Lilly; MJB (dj).

A 39.1.c
Third printing: New York: Scribners, [1974]. On copyright page: '3 . . . 19 C/C 20 . . . 2'.

A 39.2
Second edition

Bits of Paradise | 22 UNCOLLECTED STORIES BY | F. SCOTT AND ZELDA | FITZGER-ALD | Selected by | Matthew J. Bruccoli | with the assistance of | Scottie Fitzgerald Smith | PUBLISHED BY POCKET [kangaroo] BOOKS NEW YORK

1976. #80250. Wrappers. First book publication for "Dice, Brass Knuckles & Guitar."

A 39.3
Third edition

Bits of Paradise | Twenty-one Uncollected Stories by | F. Scott and Zelda Fitzgerald | Selected by | Scottie Fitzgerald Smith and | Matthew J. Bruccoli | with a foreword by | Scottie Fitzgerald Smith | Penguin Books

Harmondsworth, 1976. ISBN 0 14 00.4071 4. Wrappers.

Dust jacket for A 39.1.b

A 40 PREFACE TO THIS SIDE OF PARADISE
First edition, only printing (1975)

F. SCOTT FITZGERALD'S

PREFACE TO

THIS SIDE OF PARADISE

Edited by John R. Hopkins

The Windhover Press, Iowa City
and Bruccoli Clark, 1975

A 40: 11¾″ x 6½″

Copyright page: 'Copyright © 1975 by Frances Fitzgerald Smith'.

[1–24]

[1–3]⁴

Contents: pp. 1–4: blank; p. 5: half title; p. 6: blank; p. 7: title; p. 8: copyright; p. 9: drawing of Fitzgerald by John Thein glued to blank; p. 10: blank; p. 11: 'EDITORIAL NOTE'; p. 12: blank; p. 13: text; p. 14: blank; p. 15: text; p. 16: blank; p. 17: textual apparatus; p. 18: blank; p. 19: 'COLOPHON'; pp. 20–24: blank.

Typography and paper: 8⅞" x 3¹³⁄₁₆". 'One hundred and fifty copies have been printed from handset Palatino types on Rives Heavy, a French mould-made paper.'

Binding: Gray olive (#110) V cloth (smooth). Yellow gray (#93) label on front, printed in black: 'F. SCOTT FITZGERALD'S | PREFACE TO | THIS SIDE OF PARADISE'. Yellow gray endpapers. Top edge trimmed.

Publication: 150 copies. Published 17 December 1975. $7.75

Printing: Printed by the Windhover Press, Iowa City, Iowa. Bound by the Black Oak Bindery, Iowa City.

Location: MJB.

A 41 THE CRUISE OF THE ROLLING JUNK
First edition, only printing (1976)

The Cruise of the Rolling Junk

F. Scott Fitzgerald

Bruccoli Clark · 1976
Bloomfield Hills, Michigan
Columbia, South Carolina

A 41: 14⅜" x 10"

[A–E] 24–25 58 62 64 66; 42–43 58 72 74 76; 40–41 58 66 68 70 [71]

$[1-3]^4$

Contents: p. A: title; p. B: copyright; p. C: half title; p. D: blank; p. E: 'Introduction' signed 'M.J.B.'; pp. 24–66: text, Part One; pp. 42–76: text, Part Two; pp. 40–70: text, Part Three; p. 71: blank.

Typography and paper: Facsimile of pages from *Motor;* see C 133. Wove paper.

Binding: Gray yellow (#90) V cloth (smooth). Front: '[dark yellow brown (#78)] The Cruise | of the | Rolling Junk | F. Scott | Fitzgerald'. Light yellow brown (#76) endpapers. All edges trimmed.

Dust jacket: Printed on pale orange yellow (#73). Front: '[black] The Cruise of the Rolling Junk | [sepia photo of F. Scott and Zelda Fitzgerald with car within broken circular light brown (#57) frame] | [black] F. Scott Fitzgerald | Bruccoli Clark'. Spine, back, and flaps blank.

Publication: 1,000 copies. Published 1 May 1976. $25.

Printing: Printed by Pontiac Graphics, Pontiac, Mich. Bound by American Graphics, Philadelphia, Pa.

Locations: Lilly; MJB (dj); NjP.

Review copy: Unbound sheets with Xeroxed white label on half title: '[typed] Author: F. Scott Fitzgerald | Title: The Cruise of the Rolling Junk | Binding: Cloth over boards, with two-color dust jacket | Price: $25.00 | Publication date: 1 May 1976'. Location: MJB.

The Cruise of the Rolling Junk

F. Scott Fitzgerald

Bruccoli Clark

Dust jacket front for A 41

A 42 THREE COMRADES

A 42.1.a
First edition, only printing [1978]

F. Scott Fitzgerald's

Screenplay for

Three
Comrades

By

Erich Maria Remarque

Edited, with an Afterword by
Matthew J. Bruccoli

SOUTHERN ILLINOIS UNIVERSITY PRESS
Carbondale and Edwardsville
Feffer & Simon, Inc., London and Amsterdam

A 42.1.a: 8⅜″ x 5⅜″

Library of Congress Cataloging in Publication Data

Fitzgerald, Francis Scott Key, 1896-1940.
    F. Scott Fitzgerald's screenplay for Three comrades.

    (Screenplay library)
    "Fitzgerald's movie work": p.
    I. Bruccoli, Matthew Joseph, 1931-
    II. Remarque, Erich Maria, 1869-1970. Drei Komraden. III. Three comrades.
    [Motion picture] IV. Title. V. Title: Three Comrades. VI. Series.
    PN1997.T47   1978   813'.5'2   77-28077
    ISBN 0-8093-0854-1
    ISBN 0-8093-0853-3 pbk.

    © 1938 Loew's Incorporated. Copyright renewed 1965 by Metro-
Goldwyn-Mayer Inc. (formerly known as Loew's Incorporated).

    Published by special arrangement with Metro-Goldwyn-Mayer and Mrs.
Paulette Goddard Remarque

    Afterword by Matthew J. Bruccoli copyright © 1978 by Southern Illinois
University Press

    The screenplay by F. Scott Fitzgerald is based upon the novel *Three*
Comrades by Erich Maria Remarque, copyright © 1936, 1937 by Little
Brown & Co.; copyright renewed 1964, 1965 by Erich Maria Remarque.

    Designed by Gary Gore

Published simultaneously in cloth and wrappers.

[i–ix] x–xi [xii–xiv] [1–3] 4–252 [253–255] 256–269 [270] 271–289 [290]

Cloth: $[1–8]^{16}$ $[9]^8$ $[10]^{16}$; wrappers: perfect binding.

Contents: p. i: SIU Press logo; p. ii: series editors; p. iii: title; p. iv: copyright; p. v: contents; p. vi: blank; p. vii: acknowledgments; p. viii: blank; p. ix–xi: 'Preface | *By* Irwin R. Blacker'; p. xii: blank; p. xiii: 'EDITORIAL NOTE'; p. xiv: blank; p. 1: screenplay title page; p. 2: cast; pp. 3–252: text, headed 'Three Comrades'; p. 253: '*Afterword* | *Appendixes';* p. 254: blank; pp. 255–269: 'Afterword | *By* Matthew J. Bruccoli'; pp. 270–289: 'Appendix A | Revisions'; p. 290: 'Appendix B | Fitzgerald's Movie Work'.

Typography and paper: 6⅜" (6⅝") x 3¹⁵⁄₁₆" . Running heads: rectos, '*A Screenplay';* versos, '*Three Comrades'.* Wove paper.

Cloth binding: Deep reddish orange (#36) V cloth (smooth). Spine: '[vertically] *Fitzgerald* Three Comrades Southern Illinois University Press'. Dark grayish blue endpapers. All edges trimmed. Red and yellow bands at top and bottom.

Dust jacket: Front: '[within black frame] [section of movie poster in white, orange, yellow, brown, and green]'. Spine and back printed on orange. Spine: '[vertically] [white] THREE COMRADES [black] F. Scott Fitzgerald | [horizontally, white] [SIU Press logo]'. Back: '[black] F. Scott Fitzgerald's | Screenplay for | [white] THREE | COMRADES | [black] By ERICH MARIA REMARQUE | [white] A Screenplay | [black] Preface by | Irwin R. Blacker | Edited, with an Afterword by | Matthew J. Bruccoli | ISBN 0-8093-0854-1'. Front and back flaps have note on Fitzgerald and 3C.

Wrappers: Front same as dust jacket. Spine same as dust jacket, except that SIU Press logo is black. Back same as dust jacket, except for last line: 'ISBN 0-8093-0853-3'.

Printing: Composed by Dixie Electrotype, Nashville, Tenn. Printed and bound by Vail-Ballou, Binghampton, N.Y.

Dust jacket for A 42.1.a

Publication: 5,000 copies: clothbound, 2,000; paperbound, 3,000. Published 26 June 1978. Clothbound, $10; paperbound, $3.95.

Locations: LC (MAY 18 1978); MJB (cloth in dj and wrappers).

Review copy: Xeroxed page proofs in white covers with black plastic comb binding; off-white label printed in black on front: '[boxed SIU Press logo] | SOUTHERN ILLINOIS UNIVERSITY PRESS | Post Office Box 3697 | Carbondale, Illinois 62901 | [leaf] *We submit herewith for review* | [typed] F. SCOTT FITZGERALD'S | [printed] TITLE [typed] SCREENPLAY FOR ERICH MARIA | REMARQUE'S THREE COMRADES | [printed] AU-THOR [typed] F. Scott Fitzgerald | [printed] PUBLICATION DATE [typed] June 26, 1978 | [printed] PRICE [typed] cloth $10.00 | paper $3.95 | [printed] *We shall appreciate receiving a copy of any notice that may appear.*' Location: MJB.

A 42.2
Second edition

F. Scott Fitzgerald's | Screenplay for | THREE COMRADES | *by* Erich Maria Remarque | *Edited, with an Afterword by* Matthew J. Bruccoli | Popular Library Screenplay Series | POPULAR LIBRARY • NEW YORK

1979. ISBN 0-445-04410-1. Wrappers.

A 43 NOTEBOOKS

A 43.1.a
First edition, first printing [1978]

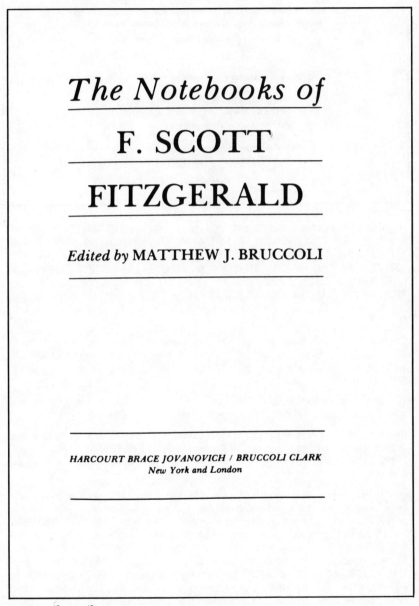

The Notebooks of

F. SCOTT

FITZGERALD

Edited by MATTHEW J. BRUCCOLI

HARCOURT BRACE JOVANOVICH / BRUCCOLI CLARK
New York and London

A 43.1.a: 8¹⁵⁄₁₆″ x 5¹⁵⁄₁₆″

Library of Congress Cataloging in Publication Data

Fitzgerald, Francis Scott Key, 1896-1940.
The notebooks of F. Scott Fitzgerald.
I. Bruccoli, Matthew Joseph, 1931-   II. Title.
PS3511.I9N6   818'.5'203   78-7954
ISBN (Harcourt Brace Jovanovich) 0-15-167260-1
♦ ISBN (Bruccoli Clark) 0-89723-001-9

First edition

B C D E

[A–D] [i–iv] v–x [xi–xiv] [1–2] 3–5 [6–8] 9–10 [11–12] 13–26 [27–28] 29–48 [49–50]
51–60 [61–62] 63–66 [67–68] 69–83 [84–86] 87–96 [97–98] 99–114 [115–116]
117–137 [138–140] 141–153 [154–156] 157–163 [164–166] 167–174 [175–176]
177–186 [187–188] 189–206 [207–208] 209–210 [211–212] 213 [214–216] 217–252
[253–254] 255–256 [257–258] 259–271 [272–274] 275–276 [277–278] 279 [280–
282] 283–291 [292–294] 295–306 [307–308] 309–336 [337–340] 341–359 [360–366]

[1–12]¹⁶

Contents: pp. A–D: blank; p. i: half title; p. ii: blank; p. iii: title; p. iv: copyright; pp. v–
vi: contents; pp. vii–x: 'Introduction'; p. xi: half title; p. xii: blank; p. xiii: 'CLASSIFICA-
TION OF NOTES'; p. xiv: blank; p. 1: 'Anecdotes'; p. 2: blank; pp. 3–359: text; pp.
360–366: blank.

Typography and paper: 6⁷⁄₁₆" (7") x 4¼" (ragged right). Running heads: rectos and
versos, *'The Notebooks of F. Scott Fitzgerald* [folio]'. Wove paper.

Binding: Medium purple (#223) V cloth (smooth). Spine stamped in deep purple
(#219): '[vertically] *The Notebooks of* | [rule] | F. SCOTT FITZGERALD | [upper right]
HARCOURT BRACE JOVANOVICH | BRUCCOLI CLARK'. White endpapers. All edges
trimmed.

Dust jacket: Front, spine, and back printed in pale yellow (#89) on deep purple blue
(#197). Front: '[within 3-sided single-rule frame, bottom rule decorated] [photo of Fitz-
gerald at desk within single-rule frame] | The Notebooks *of* | F. SCOTT | FITZGERALD |
[rule] | The first publication of the complete Notebooks | —a treasury for all readers, | a
companion for Fitzgerald enthusiasts | [ruled] | EDITED BY MATTHEW J. BRUCCOLI'.
Spine: '[vertically] The Notebooks *of* | F. SCOTT FITZGERALD | [decorated rule] |
MATTHEW J. BRUCCOLI, EDITOR | [horizontally] [HBJ device] | HARCOURT | BRACE |
JOVANOVICH | [rule] | BRUCCOLI | CLARK'. Back: '[between single vertical rules]
From | The Notebooks: | [rule] | [7 entries set off by single rules] | 0-15-167260-1'. Flaps

The Notebooks of
F. SCOTT FITZGERALD

MATTHEW J. BRUCCOLI, EDITOR

From The Notebooks:

"As a novelist I reach out to the end of all man's variance, all man's villainy—as a man I do not go that far. I cannot claim honor—but even the knights of the Holy Grail were only striving for it, as I remember."

"Ernest would always give a helping hand to a man on a ledge a little higher up."

"But he never forgot—he was forever haunted by the picture of the girl floating slowly out over the city at dusk, buoyed up by dolls, was air, by a quintessence of golden hope, like a soaring and immedia stick ascension."

"Death in most countries is considered practically fatal."

"The purpose of a fiction story is to create passionate curiosity and then to gratify it unexpectedly, orgasmically. Isn't that what we expect from all contacts?"

"I left my capacity for hoping on the little roads that led to Zelda's sanitarium."

0-15-167280-1

Jacket design copyright © 1978 by Robert Anthony, Inc.

Harcourt Brace Jovanovich/ Bruccoli Clark
757 Third Avenue, New York, N.Y. 10017

(Continued from front flap)

Fitzgerald, but whatever the mythmakers may say, the record shows that Fitzgerald was a dedicated artist and a hard-working professional. He created two profound novels in American literature, THE GREAT GATSBY and TENDER IS THE NIGHT, and over 160 short stories—including the classics "The Diamond as Big as the Ritz," "The Rich Boy," and "Babylon Revisited."

Like the Gatsby, F. Scott Fitzgerald possessed "a heightened sensitivity to the promises of life." The quality of his response and the evidence of his piercing intelligence are richly documented in these complete NOTEBOOKS.

Matthew J. Bruccoli, Jefferies Professor of English at the University of South Carolina, is the leading Fitzgerald authority. His most recent book is SCOTT AND ERNEST.

The Notebooks of F. SCOTT FITZGERALD

EDITED BY MATTHEW J. BRUCCOLI

The first publication of the complete Notebooks
—a treasury for all readers,
a companion for Fitzgerald enthusiasts

EDITED BY MATTHEW J. BRUCCOLI

$12.95

The Notebooks of F. SCOTT FITZGERALD

EDITED BY MATTHEW J. BRUCCOLI

"The more that comes to light about F. Scott Fitzgerald, the more impressive his creative effort becomes. The complete NOTEBOOKS give an inspiring view of his genius. They should be a Bible for all writers. But one does not have to be a writer to respond to these NOTEBOOKS—they make writers of us all."

—James Dickey

In 1932 one of America's most brilliant writers began a notebook, which he maintained until his death eight years later. In his NOTEBOOKS F. Scott Fitzgerald preserved the ideas, epigrams, descriptions, conversations, and witticisms—as well as passages stripped from his stories—that continued his literary labors. These 2,083 entries, which Fitzgerald organized into 23 categories—to which has been appended a section of Hollywood notes—are a treasury of autobiography, humor, pathos, and insight, providing a documentary record of the life and work of Fitzgerald during the years of his breakdown and comeback. More than anything else, the complete NOTEBOOKS reveal why he thought of himself as "the last of the novelists."

Success came early for F. Scott Fitzgerald at the age of 23 with the publication of THIS SIDE OF PARADISE in 1920—the novel that inaugurated the Jazz Age. The next twenty years were tumultuous and heartbreaking for Scott and Zelda

(Continued on back flap)

Dust jacket for A43.1.a

printed in black on white. Front flap has blurb by James Dickey and editorial blurb continued on back flap with note on editor.

Publication: 5,000 copies. Published 23 October 1978. $14.95.

Printing: Composed by BC Research, Columbia, S.C. Printed and bound by Book Press, Brattleboro, Vt.

Locations: LC (NOV 13 1978); Lilly; MJB (dj); NjP.

Note: 5 excerpts from the *Notebooks* appear in *The Bruccoli Clark News,* I (May 1978), 1.

Review copy A: Xeroxed page proofs in 2 volumes, both in strong reddish orange (#35) coated paper covers with black plastic comb binding; printed label on front: '[all the following on three panels within blue border] [on yellow panel printed in black] BRUCCOLI CLARK PUBLISHERS | 1700 LONE PINE ROAD | BLOOMFIELD HILLS, MICHIGAN 48013 | [black rule] | [on white panel] [blue] *To:* | [typed in black] THE NOTEBOOKS OF | F. SCOTT FITZGERALD | Part I [II] | [black printed rule] | [typed on yellow panel] *To be published October 1978'*. Location: MJB.

Review copy B: Xeroxed page proofs perfect-bound in brilliant purplish blue (#195) wrappers; printed on front in black: 'UNCORRECTED PROOF | *The Notebooks of* | [rule] | F. SCOTT | [rule] | FITZGERALD | [rule] | *Edited by* MATTHEW J. BRUCCOLI | [rule] | *Jefferies Professor of English, University of South Carolina* | [rule] | *HARCOURT BRACE JOVANOVICH* [slash] *BRUCCOLI CLARK* | *New York and London* | [rule]'. Manufactured by the Crane Duplicating Service, Barnstable, Mass. Location: MJB.

A 43.1.b
Second printing: New York & London: Harcourt Brace Jovanovich / Bruccoli Clark, [1978]. On copyright page: 'BCDE'. 3,500 copies.

A 43.1.c
Third printing: New York & London: Harcourt Brace Jovanovich / Bruccoli Clark, [1978]. On copyright page: 'CDE'. 2,500 copies.

A 43.1.d
Fourth printing: New York & London: Harcourt Brace Jovanovich / Bruccoli Clark, [1980]. On copyright page: 'First Harvest edition 1980'. Wrappers.

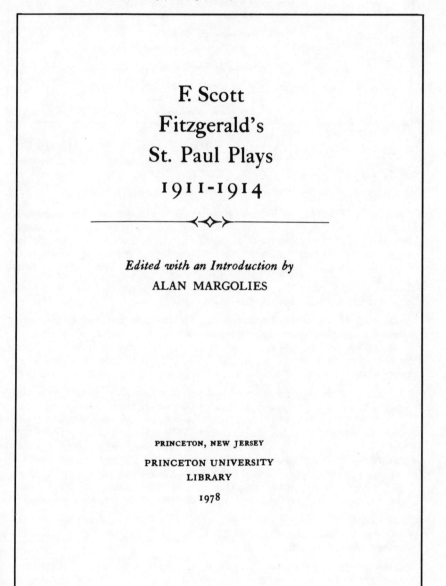

F. Scott
Fitzgerald's
St. Paul Plays
1911-1914

Edited with an Introduction by
ALAN MARGOLIES

PRINCETON, NEW JERSEY

PRINCETON UNIVERSITY
LIBRARY

1978

A 44: 8¹⁵⁄₁₆″ x 5¹⁵⁄₁₆″

[i–iv] v [vi] vii [viii] [1–2] 3–10 [11–12] 13 [14] 15–19 [20–22] 23–53 [54–56] 57–86 [87–88] 89 [90] 91–117 [118–120] 121–166 [167–168]; 8 pages of photos between pp. 72 and 73.

[1–2]^{16} [3]^{8} [4]^{4} [5–7]^{16}

Contents: p. i: half title; p. ii: blank; p. iii: title; p. iv: copyright; p. v: 'Acknowledgements'; p. vi: blank; p. vii: 'Contents'; p. viii: blank; p. 1: half title; p. 2: blank; pp. 3–10: 'Introduction'; p. 11: section title; p. 12: blank; pp. 13–117: text; p. 118: blank; p. 119: section title; p. 120: blank; pp. 121–166: textual apparatus; pp. 167–168: blank.

Four plays: The Girl from Lazy J, The Captured Shadow, Coward, Assorted Spirits.

Typography and paper: 6¾″ (7¼″) x 4⁵⁄₁₆″; 40 lines per page. Running heads: rectos and versos, play titles or section titles. Wove paper.

Binding: Light olive (#106) V cloth (smooth). Spine goldstamped: '[vertically] [2 ornaments and vertical rule] [on dark olive green (#126) panel] MARGOLIES Fitzgerald's St. Paul Plays [vertical rule and 2 ornaments]'. Strong yellow (#84) endpapers and single white binder's leaf inserted front and back. All edges trimmed. Green and yellow bands at top and bottom.

Dust jacket: Front: '[yellow gray (#93) on medium olive green (#125) panel with yellow gray single-rule frame against deep yellow (#85) border] F. Scott | Fitzgerald's | St. Paul Plays | 1911–1914 | [portrait of Fitzgerald within circle of deep yellow and yellow gray frames with yellow gray ornaments] | *Edited with an Introduction by* | ALAN MARGOLIES'. Spine [vertically, lettered in deep olive green (#126) on deep yellow] MARGOLIES [horizontal yellow gray rule] Fitzgerald's St. Paul Plays'. Back: '[lettered in deep olive green on deep yellow] PRINCETON UNIVERSITY LIBRARY | PUBLICA-TIONS | [yellow gray rule] | [5 titles] | [yellow gray rule] | [address of library]'. Flaps, printed in deep olive green and deep yellow on yellow gray, have editorial blurb with note on editor.

Publication: 2,500 copies. Published 23 October 1978. $12 ($8.50 for Friends of the Princeton University Library).

Printing: Printed by Princeton University Press. Bound by Short Run Bindery, Medford, N.J.

Locations: LC (OCT 25 1978); MJB (dj); NjP (dj).

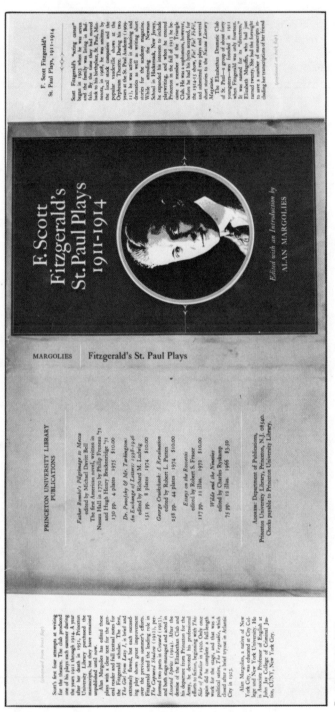

F. Scott Fitzgerald's St. Paul Plays 1911-1914

Edited with an Introduction by
ALAN MARGOLIES

MARGOLIES · Fitzgerald's St. Paul Plays

PRINCETON UNIVERSITY LIBRARY
PUBLICATIONS

Father Bombo's Pilgrimage to Mecca
edited by Michael Davitt Bell
The first American novel, written in
Nassau Hall in 1770 by Philip Freneau '71
and Hugh Henry Brackenridge '71
130 pp. 4 plates 1975 $10.00

*Dr. Panofsky & Mr. Tarkington:
An Exchange of Letters: 1938-1946*
edited by Richard M. Ludwig
151 pp. 8 plates 1974 $10.00

George Cruikshank: A Revaluation
edited by Robert L. Patten
258 pp. 44 plates 1974 $10.00

Essays on the Rossettis
edited by Robert S. Fraser
117 pp. 11 illus. 1972 $10.00

Wilde and the Nineties
edited by Charles Ryskamp
75 pp. 12 illus. 1966 $3.50

Assume: Department of Publications,
Princeton University Library, Princeton, N.J. 08540.
Checks payable to Princeton University Library.

F. Scott Fitzgerald's
St. Paul Plays, 1911-1914

Scott Fitzgerald's "acting career" began in 1903 when he was seven and the family was living in Buffalo. By the time they had moved back to his birthplace, St. Paul, Minnesota, in 1908, he was smitten by the local stock companies and the popular vaudeville, shown at the Orpheum Theatre. During his two years at the St. Paul Academy (1909-11), he was active in debating and dramatics as well as writing short stories for the academy magazine. While attending the Newman School in Hackensack, New Jersey, he expanded his interests to include playwriting, and when he entered Princeton in the fall of 1913 he became a member of the Triangle Club. His most sophomoric humor, however, before he had his lyrics accepted, for the 1914-15 show, *Fie! Fie! Fi-Fi!*, and submitted two plays and several short stories to the Nassau Literary Magazine.

The Elizabethan Dramatic Club of St. Paul—a group of about forty youngsters—was founded in 1911 when Fitzgerald was only fourteen. It was named for its "directress," Elizabeth Magoffin, who had just turned twenty. She had the foresight to save a number of manuscripts including her transcriptions of her friend

(continued on back flap)

(continued from front flap)

Scott's first four attempts at writing for the theatre. The club produced one of his plays each summer during the years 1911 through 1914. A year after her death in 1921, Princeton University Library purchased the manuscripts, but they have remained unpublished until now.

Alan Margolies has edited these plays with a clear text for the general reader and full textual notes for the Fitzgerald scholar. The first, *The Girl from Lazy J*, is brief and extremely flawed, but each succeeding play shows great improvement over the previous summer's efforts. Fitzgerald acted the leading role in *The Captured Shadow* (1912), performed two parts in *Coward* (1913), and both stage-managed and acted in *Assorted Spirits* (1914). After the demise of the Elizabethan Club and his departure from Princeton for the Army, he devoted his professional efforts to fiction, beginning with *This Side of Paradise* in 1920. Only once again did he complete a full-length work for the stage, and that was a political satire, *The Vegetable*, which closed after a brief tryout in Atlantic City in 1923.

Alan Margolies, a native of New York City, was educated at City College and New York University. He is Associate Professor of English at John Jay College of Criminal Justice, CUNY, New York City.

Dust jacket for A44

A 45 THE PRICE WAS HIGH

A 45.1.a
First edition, first printing [1979]

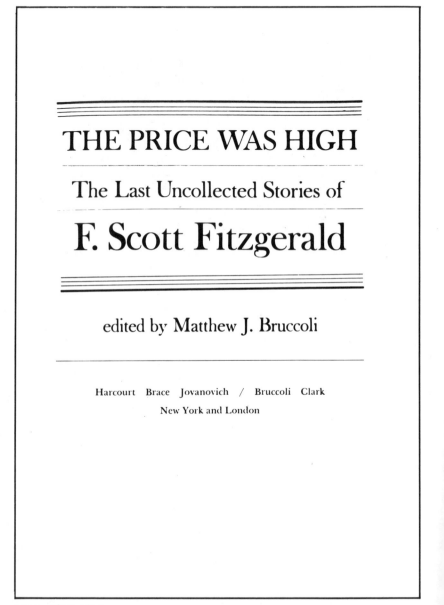

THE PRICE WAS HIGH

The Last Uncollected Stories of

F. Scott Fitzgerald

edited by Matthew J. Bruccoli

Harcourt   Brace   Jovanovich   /   Bruccoli   Clark
New York and London

A 45.1.a: 9³⁄₁₆″ x 6¹⁄₁₆″

Library of Congress Cataloging in Publication Data
Fitzgerald, Francis Scott Key, 1896-1940.
The price was high.
Includes bibliographical references.
I. Bruccoli, Matthew Joseph, 1931-   II. Title.
PZ3.F5754Pr [PS3511.I9] 813'.5'2 78-14074
ISBN 0-15-174020-8

First edition

B C D E

Copyright Acknowledgments

[i–x] xi–xx [1–3] 4–785 [786–788]; first page of each story unnumbered; 8 pages of illustrations between pp. 364 and 365.

[1–23]^{16} [24]^8 [25–26]^{16}

Contents: p. i: half title; p. ii: blank; p. iii: card page; p. iv: epigraph; p. v: title; pp. vi–viii: copyright; pp. ix–x: contents; pp. xi–xx: '$106,585'; p. 1: half title; p. 2: blank; pp. 3–784: text; p. 785: 'Editorial Note'; pp. 786–788: blank.

50 stories: "The Smilers," "Myra Meets His Family," "Two For a Cent," "Dice, Brassknuckles & Guitar," "Diamond Dick and the First Law of Woman," "The Third Casket," "The Pusher-in-the-Face," "One of My Oldest Friends," "The Unspeakable Egg," "John Jackson's Arcady," "Not in the Guidebook," "Presumption," "The Adolescent Marriage," "Your Way and Mine," "The Love Boat," "The Bowl," "At Your Age," "Indecision," "Flight and Pursuit," "On Your Own," "Between Three and Four," "A Change of

Class," "Six of One—," "A Freeze-Out," "Diagnosis," "The Rubber Check," "On Schedule," "More than Just a House," "I Got Shoes," "The Family Bus," "In the Darkest Hour," "No Flowers," "New Types," "Her Last Case," "Lo, the Poor Peacock!" "The Intimate Strangers," "Zone of Accident," "Fate in Her Hands," "Image on the Heart," "Too Cute for Words," "Inside the House," "Three Acts of Music," " 'Trouble,' " "An Author's Mother," "The End of Hate," "In the Holidays," "The Guest in Room Nineteen," "Discard" ["Director's Special"], "On an Ocean Wave," "The Woman from Twenty-One." "On Your Own" was previously unpublished; see C 336‡. First book publication for all except "Two For a Cent," "Dice, Brassknuckles & Guitar," "The Pusher-in-the-Face," "One of My Oldest Friends," "John Jackson's Arcady," "The Bowl," "At Your Age," "Flight and Pursuit," "Three Acts of Music," and "The Woman from Twenty-One."

Typography and paper: 7" (7⅝") x 4⅛"; 43 lines per page. Running heads: rectos and versos, story titles. Wove paper.

Binding: Medium yellow brown (#77) goldstamped V cloth (smooth). Spine: '[vertically] F. Scott Fitzgerald | Harcourt Brace Jovanovich [slash] Bruccoli Clark [right] [4 rules] | THE PRICE WAS HIGH | [4 rules]'. Back: '0-15-174020-8'. White endpapers. All edges trimmed. Brown and white bands at top and bottom.

Dust jacket: Printed in deep purple blue (#201) on pale brownish pink. Front: '[profile drawing of Fitzgerald in medium brown (#58) | *The Price* | *Was High* | [rule] | THE LAST UNCOLLECTED STORIES OF | *F. Scott Fitzgerald* | [rule] | EDITED by MATTHEW J. BRUCCOLI'. Spine: '*The Price* | *Was High* | [rule] | [profile drawing of Fitzgerald in single-rule frame] | [rule] | *THE LAST* | *UNCOLLECTED* | *STORIES OF* | *F. Scott* | *Fitzgerald* | [rule] | EDITED by | MATTHEW J. | BRUCCOLI | HARCOURT | BRACE | JOVANOVICH | [rule] | BRUCCOLI | CLARK'. Back: '*Contents* | [rule] | [list of contents] | 0-15-174020-8'. Front and back flap have editorial blurb with note on editor.

Publication: 15,000 copies. Published 22 January 1979. $19.95.

Printing: Composed by BC Research, Columbia, S.C. Printed by Murray Printing, Westford, Mass. Bound by American Book, Saddlebrook, N.J.

Locations: LC (AUG 14 1979); MJB (dj).

Review copy: Xeroxed page proofs perfect-bound in brilliant purplish blue (#195) paper covers; printed in black on front: 'UNCORRECTED PROOF | [4 rules] | THE PRICE WAS HIGH | [rule] | The Last Uncollected Stories of | [rule] | F. Scott Fitzgerald | [4 rules] | edited by Matthew J. Bruccoli | [rule] | PROBABLE PUB DATE: January 5, 1979 | PROBABLE PRICE: 19.95 CLOTH | Harcourt Brace Jovanovich [slash] Bruccoli Clark | New York and London'. Manufactured by the Crane Duplicating Service, Barnstable, Mass. Location: MJB.

A 45.1.b
Second printing: New York & London: Harcourt Brace Jovanovich / Bruccoli Clark, [1979]. On copyright page: 'BCDE'. 5,000 copies.

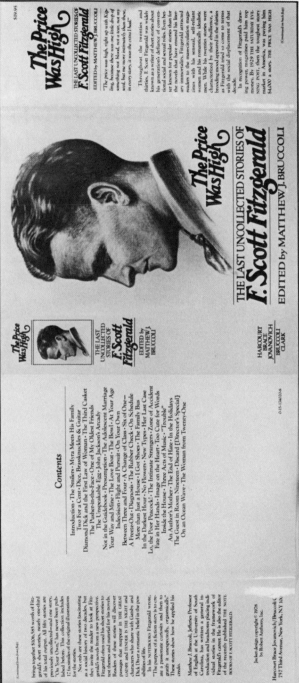

$19.95

The Price Was High

THE LAST UNCOLLECTED STORIES OF
F. Scott Fitzgerald

EDITED by MATTHEW J. BRUCCOLI

"The price was high, right up with Kipling, because there was one little drop of something not blood, not a tear, not my seed, but me more intimately than these, in every story, it was the cost I had."

Throughout the twenties and thirties, F. Scott Fitzgerald was widely known as a writer of short stories about his generation's defiance of conventional social and sexual roles. Even better known for popular stories than for the novels that have ensured his literary immortality, Fitzgerald attracted readers to the mass-circulation magazines with his sensual, self-reliant women and his romantically idealistic men. While his twenties stories were characterized by their ebullience, a brooding mood appeared in the thirties as Fitzgerald tried to come to terms with the social displacement of that decade.

In recognition of Fitzgerald's drawing power, magazines paid him top money. By 1929 THE SATURDAY EVENING POST, then the toughest story market in America, was paying him $4,000 a story. THE PRICE WAS HIGH

(Continued on back flap)

The Price Was High

THE LAST
UNCOLLECTED
STORIES OF
*F. Scott
Fitzgerald*

EDITED by
MATTHEW J.
BRUCCOLI

The Price Was High

THE LAST UNCOLLECTED STORIES OF
F. Scott Fitzgerald

EDITED by MATTHEW J. BRUCCOLI

HARCOURT
BRACE
JOVANOVICH
CLARK

0-15-173020-8

Contents

(continued from front flap)

brings together $100,585 worth of Fitzgerald's short stories, nearly one-half of his total output. All fifty stories are previously uncollected—all but one story, "On Your Own," has never been published before. This collection includes 17 facsimiles of the original illustrations for the stories.

Not only are these stories fascinating as a social history of two decades, but they are invaluable for a look at Fitzgerald's novels from a new perspective. Fitzgerald often used the short stories to test themes and material for his novels. Readers of these stories will discover passages that reappear in THE GREAT GATSBY and TENDER IS THE NIGHT and characters who share with Gatsby and Dick Diver a romantic belief in the possibilities of life.

In his notebooks Fitzgerald wrote, "The purpose of a fiction story is to create a passionate curiosity and then to gratify it unexpectedly, orgasmically." These stories show how he applied his craft.

Matthew J. Bruccoli, Jefferies Professor of English at the University of South Carolina, has written a general introduction and headnotes placing individual stories in the framework of Fitzgerald's career. He is also the editor of the recently published THE NOTE-BOOKS OF F. SCOTT FITZGERALD.

Harcourt Brace Jovanovich/Bruccoli (
757 Third Avenue, New York, NY 100

Dust jacket for A45.1.a

A 45.1.c$_1$
First English printing, first state

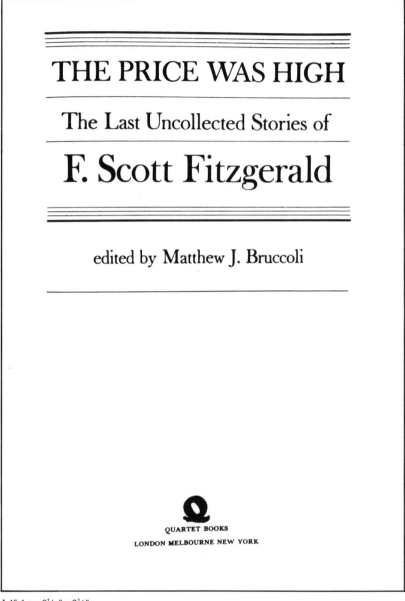

THE PRICE WAS HIGH

The Last Uncollected Stories of

F. Scott Fitzgerald

edited by Matthew J. Bruccoli

QUARTET BOOKS

LONDON MELBOURNE NEW YORK

A 45.1.c$_1$: 6^1⁄$_{16}$″ x 9^1⁄$_4$″

First published in Great Britain by Quartet Books Limited 1979
A member of the Namara Group
27 Goodge Street, London W1P 1FD

First published in the United States of America by Harcourt Brace
Jovanovich Bruccoli Clark, New York, 1979

Copyright © 1979 by Frances Scott Fitzgerald Smith
Introduction and notes copyright © 1979 by Harcourt Brace Jovanovich Inc.
Published by arrangement with Harcourt Brace Jovanovich/Bruccoli
Clark

ISBN 0 7043 2233 1

Printed and bound by The Garden City Press Limited, Letchworth,
Hertfordshire SG6 1JS

Same pagination as first printing.

[1]^8 2–51^8; p. 177 duplicates p. 162.

Contents: Same as first printing.

Typography and paper: Same as first printing.

Binding: Dark gray brown (#62) paper-covered boards with V pattern. Front has blindstamped profile of Fitzgerald. Spine goldstamped: 'Q | [rule] | [vertically] F. SCOTT FITZGERALD | THE PRICE WAS HIGH'. White endpapers. All edges trimmed.

Dust jacket: Printed in black on white. Front: '[all following within single-rule frame] THE PRICE WAS HIGH | THE LAST UNCOLLECTED STORIES OF | [rule] | F. SCOTT FITZGERALD | [rule] | [color photo of Fitzgerald within single-rule frame] | [rule] | EDITED BY MATTHEW J. BRUCCOLI'. Spine: 'THE | PRICE | WAS | HIGH | [vertically] THE LAST UNCOLLECTED STORIES OF | F. SCOTT FITZGERALD | [horizontally] EDITED BY | MAT-THEW | J. BRUCCOLI | Q | *QUARTET*'. Back blank. Blurbs on front and back flaps.

Publication: 5,000 copies of the first printing. Published 20 September 1979. £12.50.

Printing: Printed and bound by the Garden City Press Ltd., Letchworth, Hertfordshire.

Location: MJB (dj).

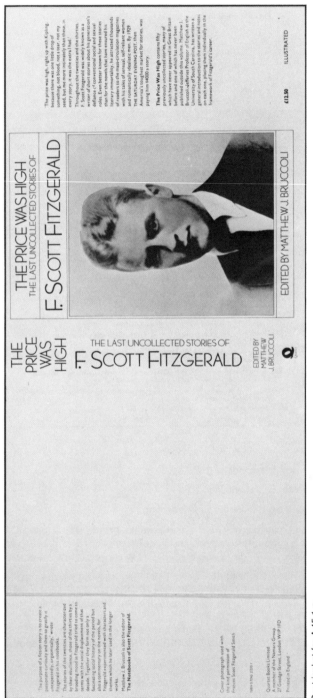

THE PRICE WAS HIGH
THE LAST UNCOLLECTED STORIES OF
F. SCOTT FITZGERALD

EDITED BY MATTHEW J. BRUCCOLI

THE
PRICE
WAS
HIGH

THE LAST UNCOLLECTED STORIES OF
F. SCOTT FITZGERALD

EDITED BY
MATTHEW
J. BRUCCOLI

The price was high, right up with Kipling, because there was one little drop of something, not blood, not a tear, not my seed, but me more intimately than these, in every story, it was the extra I had.

Throughout the twenties and the thirties, F. Scott Fitzgerald was widely known as a writer of short stories about his generation's defiance of conventional social and sexual roles. Even better known for these stories than for the novels that have ensured his literary immortality, he attracted thousands of readers to the mass-circulation magazines with his tales of sensual, self-reliant women and romantically idealistic men. By 1929 THE SATURDAY EVENING POST, then America's toughest market for stories, was paying him $4000 a story.

The Price Was High contains fifty previously uncollected stories, many of which have never appeared in Great Britain before and one of which has never been published outside this volume. Matthew J. Bruccoli, Jefferies Professor of English at the University of South Carolina, has written a general introduction to the stories and notes on each one, placing them individually in the framework of Fitzgerald's career.

£12.50   ILLUSTRATED

'The purpose of a fiction story is to create a passionate curiosity and then to gratify it unexpectedly, orgiastically,' wrote Fitzgerald in his notebooks.

The stories of the twenties are characterized by their ebullience, those of the thirties by a brooding mood as Fitzgerald tried to come to terms with the social displacement of that decade. Together they form not only a fascinating social history of the period but also a commentary on the novels, for Fitzgerald experimented with characters and themes which he later used in the longer works.

Matthew J. Bruccoli is also the editor of **The Notebooks of Scott Fitzgerald.**

Cover photograph used with the kind permission of Frances Scott Fitzgerald Smith

ISBN 0 7043 2339 1

Quartet Books Limited
A member of the Namara Group
27 Goodge Street, London W1P 1FD
Printed in England

Dust jacket for A45.1.c₁

A 45.1.c_2
First English printing, second state
[1]^8 2–12^8 13^8 (± 13 3) 14–51^8

Location: MJB (dj).

A 46 CORRESPONDENCE
Forthcoming (1980)

Correspondence of F. Scott Fitzgerald, ed. Matthew J. Bruccoli and Margaret M. Duggan, with Susan Walker. New York: Random House, 1980.

AA. Supplement

Collections

AA 5 BODLEY HEAD FITZGERALD

Volume 1 (1958) (p. 167)

Reprinted 1974.

Volume 2 (1959)

"Echoes of the Jazz Age," "My Lost City," "Ring," "Early Success," Letters to Frances Scott Fitzgerald, *TITN,* "The Last of the Belles," "A Patriotic Short," "Two Old-Timers," "An Alcoholic Case," "Financing Finnegan."

Volumes 5 and 6 (1963) (p. 168)

Adds 12 stories to contents of Cowley's *The Stories of F. Scott Fitzgerald* (1951): "The Jelly-Bean," "A Short Trip Home," "The Bowl," "Outside the Cabinet-Maker's," "Majesty," "A Night at the Fair," "He Thinks He's Wonderful," "First Blood," "One Trip Abroad," "Design in Plaster," "Boil Some Water—Lots of It," "Teamed With Genius." *No first book material.* See A 20 and A 20.2‡.

AA 8 PENGUIN STORIES

Volume 2 (p. 169)

Contents: "Echoes of the Jazz Age," "My Lost City," "Ring," "The Crack-Up," "Handle With Care," "Pasting It Together," "Early Success," "Gretchen's Forty Winks," "The Last of the Belles," "Babylon Revisited," "A Patriotic Short," "Two Old-Timers," "Financing Finnegan." Reprinted 1971, 1974 (twice).

Volume 4

Reprinted 1974.

Volume 5 (p. 170)

Reprinted 1971, 1974, 1975.

AA 12 BABYLON REVISITED
1962

Janus-sarja 5 | *F. Scott Fitzgerald* | Babylon Revisited | and | Two Other Short Stories | [device] | HELSINGISSÄ | KUSTANNUSOSAKEYHTIÖ OTAVA

Helsinki, 1962. Wrappers. "Specially adapted for the Finnish reader; Finnish vocabulary, Synonyms, Grammatical notes Idioms, etc."

3 stories: "Babylon Revisited," " 'The Sensible Thing'," and "The Baby Party."

AA 13 STORIES OF THE ROARING TWENTIES
1963

[2-page title; left:] dtv zweisprachig • Edition Langewiesche-Brandt | [right:] F. Scott Fitzgerald | Stories of the Roaring Twenties | Aus den tollen zwanziger Jahren | [boxed] dtv | Deutscher Taschenbuch Verlag

Munich, 1963. Wrappers.

3 stories: "Three Hours Between Planes," "The Dance," "A Patriotic Short." English and German on facing pages.

AA 14 THREE NOVELS
1969

"Three Novels by F. Scott Fitzgerald." Boxed set of 3 Scribner Library printings.

On copyright pages: *TSOP:* 'H-10.68 [Col]'; *B&D:* 'F-12.68 [MCOL]'; *GG:* '0-5.69 [C]'.

AA 15 LITERARY GUILD SET
1970

THIS SIDE | OF PARADISE | BY | F. SCOTT FITZGERALD | [6 italic lines] | CHARLES SCRIBNER'S SONS *New York*

.[1–11] 12–144 [145–147] 148–152 [153–155] 156–255 [256]

THE | GREAT GATSBY | BY | F. SCOTT FITZGERALD | [4 italic lines] | —THOMAS PARKE D'INVILLIERS | CHARLES SCRIBNER'S SONS *New York*

[1–7] 8–159 [160]

TENDER | IS THE NIGHT | BY | F. SCOTT FITZGERALD | [4 italic lines]—ODE TO A NIGHTINGALE | CHARLES SCRIBNER'S SONS *New York*

[1–9] 10–128 [129–131] 132–263 [264–267] 268–349 [350–352]

THE | LAST TYCOON | *An Unfinished Novel* | BY | F. SCOTT FITZGERALD | CHARLES SCRIBNER'S SONS *New York*

[1–5] 6–7 [8–9] 10–190 [191–192]

These 4 volumes were distributed by the Literary Guild of America and its associated book clubs beginning in 1970. The set was in its 17th printing by March 1973. *The Stories of F. Scott Fitzgerald* was added to the 4-volume set in 1972.

THE STORIES OF | F. Scott Fitzgerald | [decorated rule] | *A Selection of 28 Stories* | *With an Introduction by* | MALCOLM COWLEY | CHARLES SCRIBNER'S SONS *New York*

[A–B] [i–v] vi [vii] viii–xxix [xxx] [1–3] 4 [5] 6–541 [542–544]; first page of each story unnumbered.

AA 16 ABSOLUTION   MAY DAY   BABYLON REVISITED
1972

[2-page title; left:] SCOTT FITZGERALD | ABSOLUTION | MAY DAY | BABYLON REVIS-ITED | *Edited by* | A. Le Vot | *Translated by* | M.-P. CASTLENAU | *and* | B. WILLERVAL | AUBIER-FLAMMARION | [right:] SCOTT FITZGERALD | ABSOLUTION | LE PREMIER MAI | RETOUR A BABYLONE | *Introduction et Notes par* | A. Le Vot | *Traducion de* | M.-P. Castlenau | *et* | B. Willerval | AUBIER-FLAMMARION

Paris, 1972. Bilingual edition.

AA 17 SELECTED SHORT STORIES
1973

F. S. FITZGERALD e E. HEMINGWAY | SELECTED SHORT STORIES | *A CURA DI* | P. COSTA e D. CALDI | [seal] | 1973 | G. B. Petrini | TORINO

Turin. With Italian notes.

7 stories: " 'The Sensible Thing,' " "The Baby Party," "The Bridal Party," "Babylon Revisited," "Financing Finnegan," "A Patriotic Short," "Two Old-Timers."

AA 18 THE DIAMOND AS BIG AS THE RITZ
1974

Longman Structural Readers: Fiction | Stage 5 | The Diamond as Big as the Ritz | and other stories | F. Scott Fitzgerald | *Simplified and abridged by Roland John* | Illustrated by Robin Wiggins | [Longman device] | Longman

London, 1974.

7 stories: "The Diamond as Big as the Ritz," "The Long Way Out," "Bernice Bobs Her Hair," "The Baby Party," " 'The Sensible Thing,' " "The Lees of Happiness," "Gretchen's Forty Winks."

AA 19 HEINEMANN/OCTOPUS LIBRARY
1977

THE GREAT GATSBY | TENDER IS | THE NIGHT | THIS SIDE | OF PARADISE | THE BEAUTIFUL | AND DAMNED | THE LAST TYCOON | Heinemann [slash] Octopus

London, 1977.

B. First-Appearance Contributions to Books and Pamphlets

B 22 COLONIAL AND HISTORIC HOMES OF MARYLAND
Prospectus (p. 181)

An unknown number of folio signatures from the book were also circulated: p. [1]: 'Foreword' by Fitzgerald; p. [2]: blank; p. [3]: 'Acknowledgments'; p. [4]: 'Preface'.

Location: MJB.

B 23 COLONIAL AND HISTORICAL HOMES OF MARYLAND *(p. 182)*

Baltimore & London: Johns Hopkins University Press, [1975].

B 32 THE FAR SIDE OF PARADISE *(p. 185)*

Serialized in *Atlantic Monthly*, CLXXXVII (December 1950, January 1951, February 1951). Two chapters published as "Fitzgerald in the Twenties," *Partisan Review*, XVII (January 1950).

B 48 BELOVED INFIDEL *(p. 190)*

Also included in *Books Abridged* (1959?). Not seen.

B 77 CRAZY SUNDAYS *(p.199)*

London: Secker & Warburg, [1972].

B 82 THE AMERICAN CREDO
1920

THE AMERICAN CREDO | A Contribution Toward the Interpretation | of the National Mind | BY | GEORGE JEAN NATHAN | and H. L. MENCKEN | [borzoi device] | NEW YORK | ALFRED • A • KNOPF | 1920

Fitzgerald claimed the following items in his own copy (Princeton University Library): 22, 51, 193, 199, 248, 262, 429, 433, 442, 449, 450, 455.

All 12 were retained in Nathan's *The New American Credo* (New York and London: Knopf, 1927), but with changed numbers.

B 83 WIVES AND LOVERS
1956

Wives and Lovers | *edited by* | *Alex Austin* | [lion] | Lion Library | 655 Madison Avenue | New York City

1956. #LL 111. Wrappers.

"Flight and Pursuit," pp. 116–132.

B 84 LOVE AND REVOLUTION
1964

LOVE AND | [decorated rule] | REVOLUTION | [decorated rule] | *My Journey through an Epoch* | [decorated rule] | MAX EASTMAN | [decorated rule] | RANDOM HOUSE NEW YORK

1964.

On copyright page: 'First Printing'.

Letter, p. 501; reports Fitzgerald conversation, pp. 465–468.

B 85 SPELLBOUND IN DARKNESS
1966

SPELLBOUND IN DARKNESS | Readings in the History and Criticism of the Silent Film | by George C. Pratt | [5 lines of type] | University School of Liberal & Applied Studies | The University of Rochester | Rochester, New York 14627

1966; 2 volumes.

"Has the Flapper Changed?" vol. 2, pp. 385–386. See E 21.

Greenwich, Conn.: New York Graphic Society, [1973].

B 86 THE GARDEN OF ALLAH
1970

The Garden of Allah | *sheilah graham* | *crown publishers, inc., new york*

1970.

Fitzgerald verse, p. 188.

B 87 AMERICA AWAKES
1971

AMERICA AWAKES | BY | JAN FARRINGTON | a new appraisal of the Twenties | [device] | Westover | Publishing Company | an affiliate of Media General, Richmond, Virginia

1971.

Facsimiles letter and inscription to Sylvia Beach (including "Festival of St. James" drawing) in *GG*, p. 123. See B 51.

B 88 FITZGERALD AND HEMINGWAY IN PARIS
1972

F. Scott Fitzgerald and Ernest M. Hemingway | in Paris | An Exhibition | At the Bibliothèque Benjamin Franklin | In Conjunction With | A Conference At The Institut d'Études Américaines | 23–24 June 1972 | 1, place de l'Odéon | Paris, France | [device] A Bruccoli-Clark Publication | Bloomfield Hills, Michigan and Columbia, South Carolina | 1972

Wrappers. 650 copies in orange red wrappers were published for sale; 5 copies in white wrappers were not for sale.

Facsimiles inscription and letter to Van Wyck Brooks; quotes inscription to Laura Guthrie.

B 89 SCOTT FITZGERALD
1972

BY ARTHUR MIZENER | SCOTT | FITZGERALD | and his world | [T&H device] | THAMES AND HUDSON | LONDON

1972.

On copyright page: 'First Edition 1972'.

Facsimiles inscriptions.

New York: Putnam, [1972].

B 90 THE LEFT BANK REVISITED
1972

THE LEFT BANK | REVISITED: | Selections from the | Paris *Tribune* 1917–1934 | [rule] | Edited with an Introduction | by Hugh Ford | Foreword by Matthew Josephson | The Pennsylvania State University Press | University Park and London

1972.

"Fitzgerald Back from Riviera; Is Working on Novel," p. 115. See E 35‡.

B 91 FITZGERALD/HEMINGWAY ANNUAL 1972

FITZGERALD [slash] HEMINGWAY | ANNUAL | 1972 | Edited by | Matthew J. Bruccoli | *University of South Carolina* | and | C.E. Frazer Clark, Jr. | NCR MICROCARD EDITIONS

Published in Washington, D.C., 1973.

Includes the following:

"Fitzgerald on *Ulysses:* A Previously Unpublished Letter to Bennett Cerf," pp. 3–4.
R. L. Samsell, "Six Previously Unpublished Fitzgerald Letters to Hunt Stromberg," pp. 9–18.

"An Additional Fitzgerald Lyric for 'It is Art'," pp. 19–23.
"A Fitzgerald Auto-bibliography," pp. 39–41.
"Fitzgerald on 'The Ice Palace': A Newly Discovered Letter," pp. 59–60.
"10 Best Books I Have Read," pp. 67–68.
"Fitzgerald to Roger Burlingame: A New Letter," pp. 81–83.

B 92 O'HARA
1973

O'HARA | [photo] | A BIOGRAPHY | BY FINIS FARR | LITTLE, BROWN AND COMPANY—BOSTON–TORONTO

1973.

On copyright page: 'FIRST EDITION'.

Previously unpublished inscription to John O'Hara in *TITN,* quoted, p. 14. See B 93‡.

B 93 FITZGERALD/HEMINGWAY ANNUAL 1973

FITZGERALD [slash] HEMINGWAY | ANNUAL | 1973 | Edited by | MATTHEW J. BRUCCOLI | *University of South Carolina* | and | C.E. FRAZER CLARK, JR. | [device] Microcard Editions Books | An Indian Head Company | A Division of Information Handling Services

Published in Washington, D.C., 1974.

Facsimiles Fitzgerald's inscription to John O'Hara in *TITN,* front endpaper. See B 92‡.

B 94 THE ROMANTIC EGOISTS
1974

THE | ROMANTIC | EGOISTS | *EDITED BY* | MATTHEW J. BRUCCOLI | SCOTTIE FITZGERALD SMITH | *AND* | JOAN P. KERR | *ART EDITOR* | MARGARETA F. LYONS | [decoration] | *CHARLES SCRIBNERS SONS* [slash] *NEW YORK*

1974.

On copyright page: '1 . . . 19 MD/C 20 . . . 2'.

First publication of "The Pampered Men," pp. 152–153; also previously unpublished letters, inscriptions, notes.

Also 500 numbered copies signed by Scottie Fitzgerald Smith, in special binding and slipcased, with 2 color reproductions of Zelda Fitzgerald's paintings laid in.

B 95 F. SCOTT FITZGERALD
1974

F. SCOTT [thick and thin rules] | FITZGERALD | BY HOWARD GREENFELD | CROWN PUBLISHERS, INC., NEW YORK

1974.

Facsimiles *TITN* galley, p. 105.

B 96 FITZGERALD/HEMINGWAY ANNUAL 1974

FITZGERALD [slash] HEMINGWAY | ANNUAL | 1974 | Edited by | Matthew J. Bruccoli | *University of South Carolina* | and | C. E. Frazer Clark, Jr. | [device] Microcard Editions Books | An Indian Head Company | A Division of Information Handling Services

Published in Englewood, Colo., 1975.

Includes the following:

   Facsimile of Fitzgerald's inscription to Mrs. A. D. Sayre in *The Diary of Otto Braun,* front endpaper.
   "Letter to Brooks Bowman," pp. 9–10.
   Jennifer McCabe Atkinson, "The Discarded Ending of 'The Offshore Pirate'," pp. 47–49. Includes facsimile of revised TS.

B 97 THE TWENTIES
    1975

EDMUND WILSON | The Twenties | From Notebooks and Diaries | of the Period | *Edited with an Introduction by* | *Leon Edel* | [device] | FARRAR, STRAUS AND GIROUX | NEW YORK

1975.

On copyright page: 'First printing, 1975'.

Fitzgerald's song ("Dog! Dog! Dog!"), pp. 222–223. See F 99‡.

B 98 FITZGERALD/HEMINGWAY ANNUAL 1975

FITZGERALD [slash] HEMINGWAY | ANNUAL | 1975 | Edited by | Matthew J. Bruccoli | University of South Carolina | and | C.E. Frazer Clark, Jr. | [device] Microcard Editions Books | An Indian Head Company | A Division of Information Handling Services

Published in Englewood, Colo., 1975.

Includes the following:

   Facsimile of Fitzgerald's inscription to Ernest Truex in *The Vegetable,* front endpaper.
   "The Coda of 'The Swimmers'," p. 149; facsimiles revised TS.

B 99 THE REAL F. SCOTT FITZGERALD
    1976

[2-page title] [left] THE | REAL | F. SCOTT [right] FITZGERALD | [thick and thin underlines across both pages] | [left] THIRTY-FIVE [right] YEARS LATER | BY SHEILAH GRAHAM | GROSSET & DUNLAP, INC. | A FILMWAYS COMPANY | Publishers New York

1976.

On copyright page: 'First printing'.

F. Scott Fitzgerald and Sheilah Graham, "Dame Rumor," pp. 236–275. Facsimiles

Graham's story, "Not in the Script," revised by Fitzgerald, pp. 277–281. Also facsimiles poem, drawing and letters, pp. 128, 130, 134–139.

London: Allen, 1976.

[New York]: Warner, [1976]. #89-225.

B 100 PAGES
1976

[medium yellow brown] Pages | [black] THE WORLD OF BOOKS, WRITERS, AND WRITING | [medium yellow brown rule] | [black] 1 | [medium yellow brown rule] | [black] MATTHEW J. BRUCCOLI | *Editorial Director* | C. E. FRAZER CLARK, JR. | *Managing Editor* | GALE RESEARCH COMPANY • BOOK TOWER • DETROIT, MICHIGAN 48226 | [medium yellow brown rule]

1976.

Anthony Rota, "F. Scott Fitzgerald Appraises His Library," pp. 83–89; facsimiles Fitzgerald's appraisal.

B 101 FITZGERALD/HEMINGWAY ANNUAL 1976

FITZGERALD [slash] HEMINGWAY | ANNUAL | 1976 | Edited by | MATTHEW J. BRUCCOLI | University of South Carolina | Associate Editors | Margaret M. Duggan | Richard Layman | [device] Information Handling Services | An Indian Head Company | Englewood, Colorado

1978.

Includes the following:

Facsimile of Fitzgerald's inscription to Harold Ober, front endpaper.
"'Ballet Shoes': A Movie Synopsis," pp. 5–7.
Joseph Corso, "One Not-Forgotten Summer Night," pp. 8–33; facsimiles inscription in *GG* and letter to Robert Kerr.
Lloyd Hackl, "Fitzgerald in St. Paul," pp. 116–123; facsimiles *B&D* inscription and note to Oscar and Xandra Kalman; facsimiles letter to Elizabeth Clarkson Wann.
Charles Mann, "F. Scott Fitzgerald's Critique of *A Farewell to Arms*," pp. 140–153; includes Fitzgerald's letter to Hemingway.

B 102 CAST OF THOUSANDS
1977

ANITA | Cast of Thousands | LOOS | Grosset & Dunlap | Publishers • New York | A Filmways Company

1977.

On copyright page: 'First printing'.

Facsimiles holograph poem, p. 129.

B 103 THE LAST OF THE NOVELISTS
1977

"The Last of the Novelists" | F. Scott Fitzgerald and | THE LAST TYCOON | By Matthew J. Bruccoli | JEFFERIES PROFESSOR OF ENGLISH | *University of South Carolina* | SOUTHERN ILLINOIS UNIVERSITY PRESS | *Carbondale and Edwardsville* | FEFFER & SIMONS, INC. | *London and Amsterdam*

1977.

Previously unpublished material from manuscripts and notebooks. Dust jacket has 10 Fitzgerald notes on back.

B 104 IN THEIR TIME
1977

Fiestas, | *Moveable Feasts* | *and "Many Fêtes"* | in their time [slash] 1920–1940 | *An Exhibition at* | *The University of Virginia Library* | *December 1977–March 1978* | *Bruccoli Clark • 1977* | *Bloomfield Hills, Michigan* | *Columbia, South Carolina*

On copyright page: 'First Printing'.

Wrappers.

Facsimiles or quotes letters, manuscripts, and inscriptions.

B 105 FITZGERALD/HEMINGWAY ANNUAL 1977

FITZGERALD [slash] HEMINGWAY | ANNUAL | 1977 | Edited by | MARGARET M. DUGGAN | RICHARD LAYMAN | Consulting Editor: MATTHEW J. BRUCCOLI | A BRUCCOLI CLARK BOOK | GALE RESEARCH COMPANY • BOOK TOWER | DETROIT, MICHIGAN 48226

1977.

Includes the following:

Facsimile of Fitzgerald's inscription to Victoria Schulberg in *TITN,* front endpaper.
Outline and treatment for "The Feather Fan," pp. 4–8.
"The Defeat of Art," pp. 11–12. Review of Heywood Broun's *The Boy Grew Older.*

B 106 SCOTT AND ERNEST
1978

SCOTT | AND | ERNEST | The Authority of Failure | and the | Authority of Success | *Matthew J. Bruccoli* | [Random House device] | *Random House • New York*

1978.

On copyright page: 'First Edition'.

Quotes and facsimiles letters.

London, Sydney & Toronto: Bodley Head, [1978].

B 107 MAX PERKINS
1978

[within single-rule frame] MAX PERKINS | [rule] | Editor of Genius [slash] A. Scott Berg | [rule] | [caricature of Perkins by David Levine] | [rule] | *Thomas Congdon Books* TC [beehive within C] E. P. DUTTON • *New York*

1978.

On copyright page: 'First Edition'.

Letters and conversations.

B 108 FITZGERALD/HEMINGWAY ANNUAL 1978

FITZGERALD [slash] HEMINGWAY | ANNUAL | 1978 | Edited by | MATTHEW J. BRUC-COLI | RICHARD LAYMAN | A BRUCCOLI CLARK BOOK | GALE RESEARCH COM-PANY • BOOK TOWER | DETROIT, MICHIGAN 48226

1979.

Includes the following:

Fitzgerald's inscription to Gene Buck in Conrad's *Youth,* front endpaper.
"Lipstick," pp. 5–33.
Katherine B. Trower, "The Fitzgeralds' Letters to the Hoveys," pp. 55–60.
"My Ten Favorite Plays'," pp. 61–62.
"Fitzgerald's 'Favorite Story'," p. 67.

B 109 FITZGERALD/HEMINGWAY ANNUAL 1979

FITZGERALD [slash] HEMINGWAY | ANNUAL | 1979 | Edited by | MATTHEW J. BRUC-COLI | RICHARD LAYMAN | A BRUCCOLI CLARK BOOK | GALE RESEARCH COM-PANY • BOOK TOWER | DETROIT, MICHIGAN 48226

1980.

Includes the following:

Roger Lewis, "Ruth Sturtevant and F. Scott Fitzgerald (1916–1921)," pp. 3–21. In-cludes letters to Sturtevant.
"F. Scott Fitzgerald Plans a Library for Princeton," pp. 23–26. Includes facsimile of drawing.
"Fitzgerald's Revisions for 'Marching Streets'," pp. 27–29.
"Fitzgerald's Last Issue of *The Princeton Alumni Weekly,*" pp. 31–32. Includes facsi-mile of annotations.
"Fitzgerald at the Winter Carnival," pp. 35–36. Interview with Fitzgerald and Walter Wanger. See E 39.
"Fitzgerald and the *Post:* A New Letter," p. 37. Letter to Adelaide Neall.
Robert Hemenway, "Two New Fitzgerald Letters," pp. 127–128. Letters to John Franklin Carter.
"The Education of Dorothy Richardson," pp. 227–228. Reading list prepared by Fitzgerald.

BB. Supplement

Borderline Items

BB 11 IMPROMPTU CONFESSIONS
1960

[2-page title, left:] THE IMPROMPTU CONFESSIONS OF | [rule] | *Edward Anthony* | DOUBLEDAY & COMPANY, INC. | GARDEN CITY, NEW YORK | 1960 | [right:] *This is where | I came in*

On copyright page: 'First Edition'.

Conversation, pp. 129–130.

BB 12 AFTER THE GOOD GAY TIMES
1974

[2-page title] [left] Tony Buttitta | [photo of Asheville] | After | the Good [right] Gay Times | [gray] [left] *Asheville—Summer of '35* [right] *A Season with F. Scott Fitzgerald* | [black] [left] The Viking Press [slash] New York

1974.

Reconstruction of Fitzgerald conversations.

C. Appearances in Magazines and Newspapers

C1 *(p. 207)*

Addition to footnote 1: 5 unsigned limericks in *The St. Paul Academy Now and Then* are possibly by Fitzgerald: "There was a young fellow named Ware" (February 1910); "Caw Bryant's a studious boy" (February 1910); "There is an old Lady next door" (June 1910); "There is a young man who's not sour" (June 1910); "Paul Briggs is a cute little (?) lad" (June 1910). See "Fitzgerald's St. Paul Academy Publications: Possible Addenda," *Fitzgerald/Hemingway Annual 1975,* pp. 147–148.

C12 *(p. 209)*

Note: "Tiger Out To-Morrow For First Airing of Year," *Daily Princetonian* (22 October 1913), notes that the fall number of *The Princeton Tiger* included Fitzgerald's first appearance. This contribution has not been identified.

C20 *(p. 210)*

Addition to footnote 3: John McMaster has subsequently attributed "At the Field Club," *The Princeton Tiger,* XXVI (February 1916), 6, to Fitzgerald. See "As I Remember Scott," *Confrontation,* no. 7 (Fall 1973), 3–11.

C57 *(p. 216)*

"Princeton—The Last Day" was incorporated in *TSOP.*

C60 *(p. 216)*

"On a Play Twice Seen" was incorporated in *TSOP.*

C64 *(p. 217)*

"The Cameo Frame" was incorporated in *TSOP.*

C80 *(p. 219)*

"Head and Shoulders" was reprinted in England as "Topsy Turvy," *Yellow Magazine* (March 1922), 688–697. See Thomas E. Daniels, "English Periodical Publications of Fitzgerald's Short Stories: A Correction of the Record," *Fitzgerald/Hemingway Annual 1976,* pp. 124–129.

C83 *(p. 219)*

"Myra Meets his Family" was reprinted in England in *Sovereign* (July 1921), 214–226.

C84 *(p. 219)*

"The Camel's Back" was reprinted in England in *Pearson's* (February 1923), 157–164.

87

C 86 *(p. 220)*

"Bernice Bobs Her Hair" was reprinted in England in *Pan* or *20 Story*—unlocated.

C 88 *(p. 220)*

"The Offshore Pirate" was reprinted in England in *Sovereign* (February 1922), 304–315.

Note: "The Offshore Pirate" movie was adapted into a story by Donald Calhoun in *Motion Picture Classic,* XII (March 1921), 37–41, 76, 80.

C 110 *(p. 223)*

"Two For a Cent" was reprinted in England in *Argosy* (April 1933), 54–60.

C 118 *(p. 224)*

An excerpt from Fitzgerald's review, "A Rugged Novel," was used in an ad for *The Love Legend* in *Chicago Daily News* (22 November 1922), 13.

C 119 *(p. 224)*

"Winter Dreams" was reprinted in England as "Dream Girl of Spring," *The Royal Magazine,* XLIX (February 1923), 538–545, 631–636. See Thomas E. Daniels, "The Texts of 'Winter Dreams'," *Fitzgerald/Hemingway Annual 1977,* pp. 77–100.

C 126 *(p. 225)*

Excerpts from "Under Fire," Fitzgerald's review of *Through the Wheat,* were printed on the dust jackets for Boyd's *Shadow of the Long Knives* (New York: Scribners, 1928) and *Mad Anthony Wayne* (New York & London: Scribners, 1929).

C 133 *(p. 226)*

See A 41‡.

C 136 *(p. 226)*

"Gretchen's Forty Winks" was possibly reprinted in England in *Home Magazine*—unlocated.

C 137 *(p. 226)*

"What Kind of Husbands Do 'Jimmies' Make?" appeared in *Toronto Star Weekly* (29 March 1924), 24.

C 140 *(p. 227)*

"The Third Casket" was reprinted in England in *Pearson's* (November 1924), 440–448.

C 144 *(p. 228)*

"Rags Martin-Jones and the Pr-nce of W-les" was reprinted in England in *Woman's Pictorial* (18 October 1924), 6–8, 27–30.

C 145 *(p. 228)*

" 'The Sensible Thing' " was reprinted in England in *Woman's Pictorial* (22 November 1924), 13–17.

C 151 *(p. 229)*

"Love in the Night" was reprinted in England in *Woman's Pictorial* (9 May 1925), 6–9, 23–25.

C 154 *(p. 229)*

"One of My Oldest Friends" was reprinted in England in *Red Magazine* (4 June 1926), 363–372.

C 156 *(p. 229)*
"Our Young Rich Boys," *McCall's,* LIII (October 1925), 12, 42, 69.

Published with Zelda Fitzgerald's "What Became of the Flappers?" under the joint title "What Becomes of Our Flappers and Sheiks?"

Article. See A 32 and I 13‡.

Note: See p. 132 of *The Romantic Egoists* (B 94‡) for variant title.

C 157 *(p. 230)*

"A Penny Spent" was reprinted in England in *Modern Woman* (September 1926), 7–10, 48, 50, 53–54.

C 160 *(p. 230)*

"Presumption" was reprinted in England in *Woman's Pictorial* (30 November 1926), 24–27, 34, 36, 39, 40, 43.

C 161 *(p. 230)*

"The Adolescent Marriage" was reprinted in England as "The Youthful Marriage" in *Woman's Pictorial* (October 1927), 4–8, 47–48.

C 168 *(p. 231)*

(December 1927).

C 172 *(p. 231)*

"Magnetism" was reprinted in England in *Grand Magazine* August 1928), 710–722.

Note following C 183 *(p. 233)*

For a complete series of the Woodbury soap ads see *The Ladies' Home Journal* (February 1929), 107; (March 1929), 41; (April 1929), 85; (May 1929), 43; (June 1929), 71; (July 1929), 29; (September 1929), 41; (November 1929), 39; (December 1929), 29.

C 209 *(p. 236)*

Josephine story.

C 214 *(p. 237)*

"A New Leaf" was possibly reprinted in England in *Homemaking*—unlocated.

C 223 *(p. 238)*

"Flight and Pursuit" was reprinted in England in *Britannia and Eve* (June 1932), 34–37, 106–108.

C 245 *(p. 241)*

"The Fiend" was reprinted in England in *London Evening Standard* (29 March 1935), 26–27.

C 252 *(p. 242)*

"Zone of Accident" was reprinted in England as "Except to Bill," *Woman's Journal* (April 1936), 20–23, 91–93.

C 258 *(p. 243)*

"Image on the Heart" was reprinted in England as "Goodbye to Provence" in *Woman's Journal* (November 1936), 26–29, 85, 87–89.

C 274 *(p. 245)*

See F 98‡.

C 280 *(p. 245)*

In *AOAA*.

C 309 *(p. 249)*

"Last Kiss" was reprinted in England in *London Evening Standard* (1 August 1949), 8–9.

Note following C 326 *(p. 251)*

See Alan Margolies, "A Note on Fitzgerald's Lost and Unpublished Stories," *Fitzgerald/ Hemingway Annual 1972*, pp. 335–336.

C 327
The Beautiful and Damned, Metropolitan, LIV–LV (September 1921), 9–12, 55, 60–62, 65; (October 1921), 27–30, 44–49; (November 1921), 31–34, 50–52; (December 1921), 33–36, 50–54; (January 1922), 39–42, 52–55; (February 1922), 35–38, 44–47; (March 1922), 57–62, 108–109, 112–113.

Serial version. See A8 and A8‡.

C 328
"The Defeat of Art," unlocated 1922 book review of Heywood Broun's *The Boy Grew Older*.

See Margaret M. Duggan, "A New Fitzgerald Book Review: *The Boy Grew Older*," *Fitzgerald/Hemingway Annual 1977*, pp. 9–10.

C 329
"We Nominate for the Hall of Fame," *Vanity Fair*, XX (March 1923), 71.

Caption for Ring Lardner photo taken from Fitzgerald's undated letter to Edmund Wilson.

C 330
"Some Stories They Like to Tell Again," *New York Herald* (8 April 1923), magazine section, 11.

Anecdote.

C 331

"In Literary New York," *St. Paul Daily News* (23 December 1923), II, 5.

Letter to Bernard Vaughan. Replaces App. 2.14.

C 332

Tender Is the Night, Scribner's Magazine (January 1934), 1–8, 60–80; (February 1934), 88–95, 139–160; (March 1934), 168–174, 207–229; (April 1934), 252–258, 292–310.

Serial version. See A14 and A14‡.

C 333

"My Ten Favorite Plays," *New York Sun* (10 September 1934), 19.

Article.

C 334

Ad for John O'Hara's *Appointment in Samarra, New York Herald Tribune Books* (7 October 1934), VII, 17.

Includes statement by Fitzgerald. This ad was facsimiled as a keepsake by Matthew J. Bruccoli in 1972. Also reproduced in Bruccoli, *The O'Hara Concern* (New York: Random House, 1975), p. 111.

C 335

"Infidelity," *Esquire,* LXXX (December 1973), 193–200, 290–304.

Screenplay.

C 336

"On Your Own," *Esquire,* XCI (30 January 1979), 56–67.

Fiction. See A 45‡. Reprinted in [London] *Telegraph Sunday Magazine* (1 July 1979), 40–41, 43–45, 49, 52, 54.

C 337

"The Notebooks," *Antaeus,* no. 32 (Winter 1979), 101–112.

Excerpts. See A 43‡.

D. Material Quoted in Catalogues

D 8 *(p. 258)*

Recatalogued in CATALOGUE THIRTY-THREE . . . BLACK SUN BOOKS [1975]. There are 3 known copies with this inscription.

D 29 *(p. 264)*

Recatalogued in The Scriptorium [August 1972].

D 48 *(p. 268)*

Recatalogued in Doris Harris Catalogue 15 [1973].

D 49
ARGUS CATALOG NUMBER 3 . . . New York . . . [1946].

#338: TS of "The Peroxide Blonde" by Scottie Fitzgerald; each sheet signed by FSF.

D 50
Cyril Connolly's One Hundred Modern Books (Austin: Humanities Research Center, University of Texas, 1971).

#48B: Facsimiles ALS to Joseph Hergesheimer, 14 Rue de Tilsitt, Paris, n.d.: 'Dear Hergesheimer: Scribners forwarded me a copy of the letter you were kind enough to write about *The Great Gatsby*. Thank you for what you said about it as well as for the permission you so courteously gave to use your opinion. I'm afraid its a financial failure and I enclose you one of comments which may interest you. I don't do Rascoe's intelligence to think he really believes I am like Chambers—*La Cousine Bette* or *Linda Condon* could be "critisized" on the same grounds, if one wanted to make out such a preposterous case—the trouble is that we snubbed his wife. None the less I find the enclosure rather saddening review. Looking forward to *From an Old House* of which I've read with delight the three parts I came across in Italy. Again thank you, and most cordial good wishes Scott Fitzg Excuse the blots! I'm awfully anxious to see the Dower House. You promised to invite us but never did.'

D 51
Charles Hamilton AUCTION Number 55 . . . FEBRUARY 3, 1972

#158: ALS to James Rennie, Villa St. Louis, Juan-les-Pins, 17 July 1926: '. . . I sobered up in Paris and spent three days trying to get Brigham into shape. Then down here I worked on it some more and made a tentative working outline . . . I don't believe that I can make the grade and the more I struggle with it the more I'm convinced that I'll ruin your idea by making a sort of half-assed compromise between my amateur idea of "good theme" and Werner's book. I think your instinct has led you to a great idea but that my unsolicited offer was based more on enthusiasm than on common sense. So I bequeath you the notion of the girl which I think in other hands could be made quite

solid, and rather ungracefully retire hoping that Connelly or Craig will make the sort of vehicle of it that's in your imagination. It was great seeing you. You're a man after my own heart and I feel that we have by no means seen the last of each other even in a theatrical way . . . It was so nice of you to come and see Zelda. . . .'

D 52
FIRST EDITIONS modern american literature CATALOGUE FOUR [Joseph the Provider, March 1972]

#256:   *B&D,* inscribed: 'From F. Scott Fitzgerald Great-Neck, Long Island October 15, 1922.'

D 53
A MISCELLANY MODERN . . . ROMAN BOOKS, INC. . . . SCOTTSDALE, ARIZONA . . . [catalogue 7, April 1972]

#88:   *TSOP,* inscribed.

#89:   *B&D,* inscribed.

D 54
Charles Hamilton AUCTION Number 60 . . . August 3, 1972 . . .

#66-A: TLS to C. A. Wright, Baltimore, Md., 24 April 1935: 'I was on the *Tiger* staff at Princeton for three years and got out many issues . . . though I was not chairman. It was never as big a thing at Princeton as was the *Record* at Yale . . . because most of the local wit was concentrated on producing the hullabaloo of the Triangle show, and lately the "Intime" reviews. My time was chiefly notable for the first acknowledgment in print that girls would be girls and the first use in the east of such words as "necking" and "petting" exemplified by a series which I started . . . called *International Petting Cues. . . .'* See F 100‡.

D 55
Charles Hamilton AUCTION Number 61 . . . SEPTEMBER 14, 1972

#160:   LS to E. S. Oliver, Baltimore, 7 January 1934: 'The first help I ever had in writing in my life was from my father who read an utterly imitative Sherlock Holmes story of mine and pretended to like it. But after that I received the most invaluable aid from . . . headmaster of the St. Paul Academy . . . from Courtland Van Winkle in freshman year at Princeton . . . he gave us the book of *Job* to read and I don't think any of our preceptorial group ever quite recovered from it . . . Most of the professors seemed to me old and uninspired, or perhaps it was just that I was getting under way in my own field. I think this answers your question. This is also my permission to make full use of it with or without my name. . . .'

#161:   LS to E. S. Oliver, Baltimore, 1 February 1935: '. . . I don't want to be quoted . . . anything you may want to use from my letter is to be summarized. . . .'

D 56
FIFTY FOR THE FAIR HERITAGE BOOKSHOP . . . HOLLYWOOD, CALIFORNIA . . . [September 1972]

#11:   *GG,* inscribed: 'For . . . . , from an unknown admirer, F. Scott Fitzgerald. Autumn 1940'.

#12:   *ASYM,* inscribed: 'For . . . . , from F. Scott Fitzgerald, one sad young man to another. Hollywood, 1940'.

#13:   *TITN,* inscribed: 'To . . . . , from his friend F. Scott Fitzgerald, This story of a Europe that is no more. September 1940'. Recatalogued in CATALOGUE 118 . . . HERITAGE BOOKSHOP . . . [1974].

#14:   *TAR,* inscribed: 'For . . . . , with gratitude from F. Scott Fitzgerald. Armageddon, Annus I (1940 Old Style)'. Recatalogued in *J & S Catalogue 16* [1973].

D 57
AUTOGRAPHS FOR SALE * CONWAY BARKER . . . LA MARQUE, TEXAS . . . [List 724-2, 1972]

ALS to Miss Cornelia C. Abbot of Lynn, Massachusetts, Great Neck, 27 March 1924: 'The Post has sent me your accusation. I use to defend myself. (1) Baby had nurse mentioned in fourth or fifth paragraph of story. (2) Nurse found door locked, concluded Gretchen was in city & carried on. Q.E.D. Sincerely, F. Scott Fitzgerald'. Recatalogued in Thomas M. FASSETT, INC. autographs . . . [catalogue 2, 1972].

D 58
GRM Catalog 16 . . . George Robert Minkoff . . . Great Barrington, Mass. . . . [1972]

#470:   *GG,* inscribed: 'For . . . . . From us sincerely F. Scott Fitzgerald Feb. 1927'.

#471:   *ASYM,* inscribed for: '. . . with best wishes F. Scott Fitzgerald'. Includes Fitzgerald drawing captioned 'TYPICAL SAD YOUNG MEN'.

D 59
MODERN LITERATURE . . . BLACK SUN BOOKS . . . BROOKLYN, NEW YORK . . . [catalogue 10, 1972]

#110:   *B&D,* inscribed: 'For '. . . with best wishes from F. Scott Fitzgerald This was a book about things I knew nothing about, a drawing upon experiences that I had not had. Much more than my first book this was a piece of insolence.' With TLS.

D 60
SALE NUMBER 68 . . . THE FINE LIBRARY OF THE LATE INGLE BARR . . . February 18 . . . SOTHEBY PARKE BERNET, LOS ANGELES . . . [1973]

#214:   *ASYM,* inscribed to Horace McCoy: 'Paramount, 1939'.

D 61
SALE NUMBER 3476 . . . *February 20* . . . EXHIBITION AND SALE AT SOTHEBY PARKE BERNET INC. . . . 1973 [New York]

#207:   Manuscript material and ephemera connected with two girl friends of Fitzgerald's undergraduate days—Marie Hersey and Ginevra King.

1. ALS to Marie Hersey at the Westover School, 107 Patton Hall, Princeton University, Jan. 1915: '. . . The letter that you sent, Marie, | Was neither swift nor fair. | I hoped that you'd repent, Marie, | Before the start of Lent, Marie, | But Lent could not prevent Marie | From being debonnaire | . . . So write me what you will, Marie, | Altho' I will it not. | . . . And tho' you treat me ill, Marie, | Believe me I am still, Marie, | Your fond admirer | Scott.'

2. Description and partial facsimile of AL to Marie Hersey, n.p., n.d. [probably Princeton, 1915], in the form of a collage with clippings of advertisements.

3. AN headed: 'Sacred to the memory of Xmas 1911 . . . for Marie Hersey.'

4. A dance card belonging to Ginevra King on which Fitzgerald has signed his name, 'Scot Fitz', for two dances [St. Paul, Minn., Christmas 1915]. Also King's and Fitzgerald's calling cards. Also AN by Ginevra King to Fitzgerald.

Items 2, 3, and 4 recatalogued in *No. 931 London, 1973 . . . Bernard Quaritch Ltd . . .*; facsimile of additional pages of item 2 recatalogued in *AUTOGRAPH LETTERS MANU-SCRIPTS DOCUMENTS . . .* Catalogue 102 . . . *KENNETH W. RENDELL, INC.* [January 1975]. See D 74‡.

D 62
CATALOGUE 20 MODERN LITERATURE . . . BLACK SUN BOOKS . . . NEW YORK, NEW YORK . . . [May 1973]

#70: The Gateway Series of English Texts—Washington's Farewell Address and Webster's First Bunker Hill Oration (New York, 1911). Signed on the title page: 'Francis Scott Fitzgerald Newman School Hackensack New Jersey.' He has also written above the printed text of Washington's address: 'Your most humble & obedient servant, Geo. Washington'. With autobiographical comments on rear endpaper: 'With apologies for living Francis Scott Fitzgerald.'

#71: TSOP, inscribed.

D 63
SALE NUMBER 94 . . . October 21, 1973 . . . SOTHEBY PARKE BERNET, LOS AN-GELES . . .

#173: F&P, inscribed: 'For Eleanor Lindsley from F. Scott Fitzgerald. "Where have I seen her?" '

#175: TITN, inscribed: 'Dear Nancy, to you, Scott'; *VEG,* inscribed.

D 64
BERNICE WEISS, BOOKS . . . EASTCHESTER, N.Y. . . . CATALOG NUMBER 46 . . . [1973]

#177: F&P, inscribed: 'To Caroline Pfeiffer from F. Scott Fitzgerald (on a most embar-rasing occasion.)'.

D 65
Catalogue 615 MODERN FIRST EDITIONS . . . WILLIAM YOUNG AND CO. [February 1974]

#188: Holograph poem, January 1915, written on Princeton stationery giving Fitzger-ald's room number as '107 Patton Hall' and signed 'Scott'.

#189: Signed holograph poem, 1937.

Both items recatalogued in Catalogue 617 . . . WILLIAM YOUNG AND CO. [April 1975] and Catalogue 619 . . . WILLIAM YOUNG AND CO. [February 1976].

D 66
AMERICANA MAIL AUCTION   George M. Rinsland . . . Allentown, Pa. . . . AUCTION NO. 56 . . . May 25, 1974

#1190: The Diary of Otto Braun, inscribed by Fitzgerald: 'Dear Mrs. Sayre—I think you will love this book. I am simply wild about it. Scott.' See B 96‡.

D 67
SALE #127 ... June 23 ... June 24, 1974 ... SOTHEBY PARKE BERNET, LOS AN-
GELES ...

#328: TITN, facsimiles inscription: 'Dear Curtis—you've been so appreciative of my
books in the past that I thought this might amuse you Scott Fitzgerald.' Recatalogued in
SALE NUMBER 3482 ... February 25, 1976 ... SOTHEBY PARKE BERNET ... NEW
YORK.

D 68
RARE BOOKS ... BLACK SUN BOOKS [Catalogue 28, August 1974]

#97: B&D with ALS pasted to the front pastedown endpaper: 'Dear——I assure you
that its just because its such a nice name that its bound for such a fate. I'm glad to give
my signature. Clip on dotted line or something. Sincerely. F. Scott Fitzgerald. 626
Goodrich Ave   St. Paul, Minn.'

D 69
Charles Hamilton AUCTION Number 81 ... OCTOBER 10, 1974

#203: ALS to Mrs. Winter, 27 March 1922.

D 70
FIRST EDITIONS ASSOCIATION COPIES ... HOUSE OF BOOKS ... NEW YORK ...
[October 1974]

#193: TLS to Cecilia Taylor, Baltimore, 8 December 1934: 'Dearest Ceci: Thought this
might amuse you. It is a fake set up by courtesy for me by some newspaper friends. It
was a bread-and-butter letter to a friend I visited in Loudon County last summer. Don't
let it get in the real press! Love always, Scott'. With *The True Story of Appomattox.*
Recatalogued in SALE NUMBER 3966 IMPORTANT MODERN FIRST EDITIONS ...
March 29, 1977 ... SOTHEBY PARKE BERNET INC. ... NEW YORK .... See A 16
and A 16‡.

D 71
SALE NUMBER 3708 ... *December 14, 1974* ... EXHIBITION AND SALE AT SOTH-
EBY PARKE BERNET INC. ... New York ...

#577: ALS to David Balch, Westport, Conn., 19 June 1920. Most of the letter deals
with 'Head and Shoulders', which 'will be republished in my collection of short stories
"Flappers and Philosophers" which the Scribners are publishing this fall.' Fitzgerald
would 'rather watch a good shimmee dance than Ruth St. Dennis & Pavalowa com-
bined. I see nothing at all disgusting in it.' ' "The Camel's Back" in the S.E.P. (which
you may be buying) was the fastest piece of writing I've ever heard of. It is twelve
thousand words long and it was written in fourteen hours straight writing and sent to the
S.E.P. in its original form.' He has 'no good picture. I expect to have some soon though
& will send you one.'

#578: TSOP, inscribed: 'Sincerely, F. Scott Fitzgerald.'

D 72
CATALOGUE 46   1974   Modern First Editions ... John Howell ... San Francisco ...

#609: B&D, inscribed: 'Sincerely, F. Scott Fitzgerald.'

D 73
J & S Catalogue Number 20 ... [1974]

#216: F&P, inscribed: 'Yours in Xt.' Includes a small drawing by Fitzgerald of a beer stein over a cross. Recatalogued in *J & S [Graphics] Catalogue Number 21* [1974] and SALE NUMBER 3946 FINE BOOKS . . . January 20 . . . 1977 . . . SOTHEBY PARKE BERNET INC. . . . NEW YORK . . . .

D 74
AUTOGRAPH LETTERS MANUSCRIPTS DOCUMENTS Catalogue 102 *KENNETH W. RENDELL, INC.* [January 1975]

#37: Partial facsimile of ALS to Marie Hersey, n.p., n.d. [early 1915], in the form of a collage, headed *'Letter for Hersey!'* 'My heavens, who'd write to her—must be a mistake. What are the initials—M.L.—well, that's write (a pun). However I would advise Miss Hersey if she wants to keep her peace of mind and moreover her modesty not to look at middle pages of this sheet. . . . There—she turned it. . . . This is shocking! We must turn the page quickly. . . .' Fitzgerald illustrated this page with clippings of a nude woman, a bathtub, and a man in the background peering through a window. 'Ah! She's going to read while bathing—but—who is that man in the window? How *interested* he looks!' A picture of a garterbelt bears the notation: 'This is her coat-of-arms. Translation "She loves to snap 'em." ' Followed by a page dedicated to Marjorie Howey Muir. The fifth page is dedicated to Ginevra King. 'Poor Ginevra! This is some school she's going to next year! It's not a finishing school but it will be her finish! By that time she'll be well-fitted to [printed] Become a Nurse! Poor Ginevra!' On this page Fitzgerald mounted an advertisement for the Lasell Seminary for Young Women. See D 61‡.

D 75
SALE NUMBER 167 . . . May 11, 1975 . . . SOTHEBY PARKE BERNET, LOS ANGELES . . .

#229: ANS: 'For Mrs. [Ivan] Kahn with many thanks for a delightful luncheon F. Scott Fitzgerald.'

D 76
DORIS HARRIS DISTINGUISHED AUTOGRAPHS CATALOG No. 18 . . . [June 1975]

#63: 1. TLS, To Don Swann, Baltimore, ca. July 1935, noting that after publication of Swann's book, *Colonial and Historic Homes of Maryland,* all rights to Fitzgerald's preface would revert to him. He allows Swann some leeway on revisions but none '. . . that would utterly defeat the rhythm and so the purpose of the introduction. . . .'

2. ALS to Don Swann, Grove Park Inn, Asheville, ca. July 1935: '. . . The reason I didn't want the one of Hampton was because the Pleausance Ridgely from whom I am descended, antedated the present mansion by a generation & I thought it would be pretentious of me to hang it for that reason. But direct ancestors *did* live in Tudor Hall so you can imagine the pleasure it gives me. . . .' See F 88‡.

D 77
AB Bookman's Weekly, 55 (7 July 1975), 99.

TSOP, inscribed: 'For John Myers O'Hara who first introduced me to Sapho in his translations, with a thousand thanks. "Much have I travelled in the Realms of gold"? his most Cordially, F. Scott Fitzgerald, Washington D.C.' Recatalogued in FIRST EDITIONS . . . HOUSE OF BOOKS, Ltd. . . . NEW YORK . . . [1976].

D 78
Charles Hamilton AUCTION Number 89 . . . JULY 24, 1975

#130: ALS to Harry Hansen, with envelope postmarked Paris, 13 June 1925: 'Thank you for your kind letter about *Gatsby.* You have always been so nice about my stuff that I'd hoped this would please you too. Thanks for letting me know it did.'

D 79
CATALOGUE FIFTY FIRST EDITIONS . . . BERNICE WEISS, BOOKS . . . EAST-CHESTER, NEW YORK . . . [September 1975]

#245: TSOP, inscribed.

D 80
George S. MacManus Co. FINE BOOKS Catalogue 226 [1975]

#110: VEG, facsimiles inscription: 'For Kenneth Brightbill from F. Scott Fitzgerald May 4th 1922.' Recatalogued in JOSEPH THE PROVIDER . . . Santa Barbara, California . . . [Catalogue Fifteen, n.d.]. Also in SALE NUMBER 3966 IMPORTANT MODERN FIRST EDITIONS . . . March   29,   1977 . . . SOTHEBY   PARKE   BERNET   INC. . . . NEW YORK . . . .

D 81
J & S Catalogue No. 23 . . . FIRST BOOKS . . . [1975]

#124: TSOP, inscribed and dated 26 March 1920.

D 82
FIRST EDITIONS . . . HOUSE OF BOOKS, Ltd . . . NEW YORK . . . [1976]

#152: ALS to T. R. Smith (of Boni & Liveright), Paris, n.d. [1925]: 'Thanks for kind letter about *Gatsby,* afraid it is not going to sell like the others. His relations with Max Perkins and Scribners have always been so cordial he could not imagine breaking them, but if anything happens will surely come to his firm. "But it would be a monopoly in restraint of trade . . . you already have the only other two Americans under thirty who promise a great deal—Hemingway and Cummings. . . ." Will be in Paris the rest of 1925.'

D 83
SALE NUMBER 3946   FINE BOOKS . . . January 26, 1977 . . . SOTHEBY PARKE BER-NET INC . . . NEW YORK . . .

#223: ASYM, inscribed: 'For Bob Ingalls. In memory of a summer on the Baltic Sea, from his faithfully F. Scott Fitzgerald. Juan-les-Pins, 1926.'

#224: F&P, inscribed to Kenneth Brightbill. See D 73. Also in *J & S Catalogue Number 21* [1974].

#225: TSOP, inscribed: 'For Bob Ingalls from his friend F. Scott Fitzgerald, Aug. 1926.'

D 84
AB Bookman's Weekly, 59 (28 February 1977), 1376.

TITN, inscribed: 'Her-Fri(e)d Friend is Very Fond of Her, And She Will Just Half (sic) to Except His Bad Puns. F. Scott Fitzgerald 1934 The Art Museum, Philadelphia. "With Audible Screams" '. Recatalogued in *Catalog Number One Maurice F. Neville . . . Santa Barbara . . .* [1977].

D 85
SALE NUMBER 3966 IMPORTANT MODERN FIRST EDITIONS . . . March 29, 1977 . . .
SOTHEBY PARKE BERNET INC. . . . NEW YORK . . .

#105: *TSOP,* inscribed: 'For Harold Davis with Best Wishes from F. Scott Fitzgerald,
July 2nd, 1920.'

#108: *TJA,* inscribed: 'For Kenneth Brightbill from F. Scott Fitzgerald who purchased
this book for presentation to said gent. on this sunny day of September 27th, 1922'.

#110: *GG,* facsimiles inscription: 'For Rosalind and Capitan with affection from Scott
and Zelda, June (May) 1925'.

#114: *TITN,* facsimiles inscription to Malcolm Cowley: 'Dear Malcolm: Please don't
review this—I know how you'd do it. Put a young man on it—oh hell—use your own
judgement, as you will anyhow. Ever Yours, Scott'.

#117: Zelda Fitzgerald. ALS to Madeleine Boyd, Paris, ca. 2 July 1926: '. . . I swim all
day and enjoy tremendously a vague nostalgia that comes from living in a perfect
place and wishing there was somewhere to go . . . We are coming home in Nov. or
Dec.—neither Scott nor I quite know why. Perhaps to stay—Scott's writing an amaz-
ingly good novel which goes so slow it ought to be serialized in the Encyclopedia
Britannica . . . give my love to Ernest and Lewey Collins is a bitch and everybody hates
the Bromfields and life is, after all, very complicated'.

Note: 35 numbered copies of this catalogue were specially bound.

D 86
SALE NUMBER 4057 FINE BOOKS & AUTOGRAPH LETTERS . . . 6 December
1977 . . . SOTHEBY PARKE BERNET . . .

#85: *B&D,* inscribed to Harry Hansen: 'Dean of the Middle-West from his friend F.
Scott Fitzgerald'.

D 87
Fine Books from Many Fields . . . Bennett & Marshall . . . LOS ANGELES,
CALIFORNIA . . . [1977]

#63: *VEG,* inscribed.

D 88
John E. Baker, *A Catalogue of Twentieth Century Literature* . . . (Desbarats, Ontario,
1977).

#A20: ALS to Dale Burckhart, Nice, 27 March 1929.

D 89
The Collector: A Magazine for Autograph and Historical Collectors, Whole No. 854
(1977) (Walter R. Benjamin Autographs).

#K-746: TLS to Mrs. H. H. Prouse, La Paix, Rodger's Forge, Towson, Md., 18 July
1933: 'The Keys settled in Maryland with a tremendous grant about 1698 in St. Mary's
County. They were rich with no special record of service to the state until after the
Revolution. You and I are both descended from Philip Key, who died about 1800, you
through his grandson Francis Scott Key, and I through Francis Scott Key's uncle Philip
Barton Key . . . In my branch of the Key family (descendants of Philip Barton Key) there
has been no money or achievement of note for four or five generations though some of
the descendants have married well. . . . I am told here in Baltimore that two men

bearing the Key name, descendants of the aforementioned Philip Key, died poverty stricken in the Confederate Home at the beginning of the century. So I am afraid we must forget past glories, if there were any, and look forward to the future'.

D 90
AB Bookman's Weekly, 61 (9 January 1978), 293.

TLS to Robert Bennett, 28 November 1940.

D 91
Charles Hamilton AUCTION Number 111 . . . MARCH 23, 1978

#109: ALS to Arthur W. Brown, Great Neck, 15 November 1922: 'Hovey gave me an advance copy of the magazine—almost his last official act before leaving the *Metropolitan.* The drawings . . . were excellent—careful, beautifully done and "appetizing," like everything you do. If you had heard me beg Hovey in letter after letter to have you do *The Beautiful & Damned* you would know how much I appreciate your work. . . .'

#110: ALS to Brown, n.d.: '. . . I'm sorry my suggestions are so few & so fragmentary but Mr. Hovey has asked me for them right away & it has been a most peculiar story— not nearly so obvious as it sounds here. I like all your work very much and was tremendously pleased at your illustrations for *The Camel's Back* and for *The Jellybean.* . . . The story concerns a poor boy, his rise and his attempts to win a rich girl. He first sees her when he is a caddy about 14 years old. . . . The sight of her stirs the poor boy to give up his job of caddying—He is too proud to caddy for a little girl as young as that—He rises in the world. At 25 he is a guest at the golf club where he has been a caddy. She comes by in a motor boat & they go surf-board riding under the moon. . . . My other scenes do not offer much pictorial possibility. I have just destroyed the second part of the story & am doing it over again—so I hope you can get the two illustrations from the 1st page of this letter. . . .' Includes Fitzgerald's drawing indicating the characters on the golf course. In lower-right corner: 'Don't be jealous because I draw so well. F.S.F.' Fitzgerald's drawing facsimiled on p. 24.

#111: ALS to Brown, Great Neck, n.d.: 'The pictures arrived and now decorate the walls of my den together with W.E. Hill's cover for *This Side of Paradise.* They seem marvellously done to me—and the whole household (including the baby) have inspected them admiringly . . . I remember your illustrations to *Seventeen*—the big fat lummox singing for instance and the two little girls "walking with their stomachs out." They were marvellous. I shall certainly specify you for my next stuff. I don't know about The Winter Club—it would be a perpetual Sunday night temptation & I have enough already. . . .'

E. Interviews

E 1 *(p. 271)*

See A 32, E 32.

E 15 *(p. 272)*

Also noted in *St. Paul Pioneer Press* (30 September 1923), magazine section, 2.

E 17 *(p. 273)*

See A 32.

E 21 *(p. 273)*

See B 85‡

E 34

Wilson, B. F. "F. Scott Fitzgerald on 'Minnie McGluke'," *Picture-Play,* XIX (October 1923), 83–84, 102.

E 35

"Fitzgerald Back from Riviera; Is Working on Novel," *Paris Tribune* (9 April 1929), 8. See B 90‡.

E 36

Bald, Wambly. "La Vie de Boheme (As Lived on the Left Bank)," *Chicago Daily Tribune* (Paris edition) (16 December 1929), 5.

E 37

"F. Scott Fitzgerald Is Hunting Trouble," *Baltimore Evening Sun* (29 June 1932), 36.

E 38

"Fitzgeralds Felt Insecure in France; Now Live Here," *Baltimore Evening Sun* (25 October 1932), 3.

E 39

Hess, John D. "Wanger Blends Abruptness with Charm in Personality," *The Dartmouth* (11 February 1939), 2, 13. Interview with Fitzgerald and Walter Wanger. See B 109.

F. Articles That Include Material by Fitzgerald

F 88
Benjamin, Mary A. "Reading Into the Past," *Architectural Digest*, XXXIII (July/August 1976), 113.

Facsimiles letter to Don Swann.

F 89
Bruccoli, Matthew J. " 'An Instance of Apparent Plagiarism': F. Scott Fitzgerald, Willa Cather, and the First *Gatsby* Manuscript," *The Princeton University Library Chronicle*, XXXIX (Spring 1978), 171–178.

Facsimiles letter to Cather and 2 pages from first MS for *Gatsby*.

F 90
Cowley, Malcolm. "Fitzgerald's 'Tender'—The Story of a Novel," *New Republic*, CXXV (20 August 1951), 18–20.

Quotes from letters and notes; incorporated in Cowley's introduction to revised *TITN*.

F 91
Kent, Beth. "Fitzgerald A Ghostly Figure of Another Time," *Twin Citian*, X (October 1967), 15–19.

Quotes letter and reports conversation.

F 92
Latham, Aaron. "The Making of 'Crazy Sundays'," *Princeton Alumni Weekly*, LXXI (1 June 1971), 8–10.

Facsimiles page of revised TS for *LT*.

F 93
Margolies, Alan. "F. Scott Fitzgerald's Prison Play," *Papers of the Bibliographical Society of America*, LXVI, no. 1 (1972), 61–64.

Includes material from *Play* notebook.

F 94
Myers, Andrew B. " 'I Am Used to Being Dunned': F. Scott Fitzgerald and the Modern Library," *Columbia Library Columns*, XXV (February 1976), 28–39.

Includes letters to Bennett Cerf and Donald Klopfer.

F 95
The Princeton University Library Chronicle, XXXIV (Spring 1973), 183.

Reports inscribed *GG*: 'For Telulah, from her admiring friends Scott & Zelda. Paris, November 1925.'

F 96
West, James L. W., III. "The Corrections Lists for F. Scott Fitzgerald's *This Side of Paradise*," *Studies in Bibliography*, XXVI (1973), 254–264.

Quotes letters and memos.

F 97
West, James L. W., III. "F. Scott Fitzgerald to Arnold Gingrich: A Composition Date for 'Dearly Beloved'," *Papers of the Bibliographical Society of America*, LXVII, no. 4 (1973), 452–454.

Includes 23 February 1940 letter to Gingrich.

F 98
West, James L. W., III. "Notes on the Text of F. Scott Fitzgerald's 'Early Success'," *Resources for American Literary Study*, III (Spring 1973), 73–99.

Facsimiles 2 pages of TS and quotes other material. See C 274.

F 99
Wilson, Edmund. "The Twenties," *The New Yorker*, LI (28 April 1975), 58.

First publication of Fitzgerald song "Dog! Dog! Dog!". See B 97‡.

F 100
Wright, Charles A. "When Punch Bowl had some punch," *Pennsylvania Gazette*, LXXIV (November 1975), 25.

Includes 1935 letter to Wright. See D 54‡.

G. Dust-Jacket Blurbs

G 1 *(p. 291)*

An ad for *Babel* in the *Chicago Daily News* (20 September 1922), 12, has a longer version of Fitzgerald's statement. The short blurb was used for an ad in the *New York Tribune* (15 October 1922), V, 9.

H. Keepsakes

H 7 TELEGRAM KEEPSAKE
1972

Facsimile of Western Union telegram, Fitzgerald to Maxwell Perkins, 15 March 1934.

Colophon: '100 Copies Printed For Distribution At The C.E.A.A. Symposium On The Text And The Study of American Literature, The University Of Manchester, 30 June 1972. . . .'

Columbia, S.C.: Bruccoli, 1972.

Single gray yellow (#90) sheet printed on one side. 8½" × 10^{15}⁄$_{16}$".

Locations: Lilly; MJB; PSt.

H 8 F. SCOTT FITZGERALD'S PROJECTED COLLECTED WORKS
1972

Facsimile of Fitzgerald's holograph plan for his collected works.

Colophon: '300 Copies Printed To Mark Publication Of *F. Scott Fitzgerald: A Descriptive Bibliography* By Matthew J. Bruccoli. . . .'

Columbia, S.C.: Bruccoli, 1972.

Single yellow white (#92) sheet printed on one side. 8½" × 11".

Locations: Lilly; MJB; PSt.

H 9 THIS SIDE OF PARADISE KEEPSAKE
1972

On title page: '[first 4 words underlined] *This Side of Paradise, The Grammarian,* | *and the "Author's Final Intentions"* | [blue] *by* | *James L. W. West III* | *Virginia Polytechnic Institute and State University* | [5 lines in black]'.

Colophon: 'One of 100 copies. This is copy ___ .'

N.p.: West, 1972.

Single pale orange-yellow (#73) sheet printed in black and blue, folded twice to make 6 pages. 6" × 8". Facsimiles 3 pages of *TSOP* MS and TS.

Location: MJB.

H 10 GREAT GATSBY KEEPSAKE
1975

Head title: 'The Great Gatsby | 10 April 1925–10 April 1975 | An Exhibition from the Collection of | Matthew J. Bruccoli | at | THE GROLIER CLUB | 1975'.

Colophon: '300 Copies Printed For The Grolier Club Exhibition By Vogue Press, Inc., Columbia, S.C.'

Columbia, S.C.: Bruccoli, 1975.

Single light yellow (#86) sheet printed on both sides. 8″ × 23$^{15}/_{16}$″. Recto: facsimile of unrevised galley 31; verso: exhibition list.

Locations: Grolier; Lilly; MJB; PSt.

H 11 LARDNER KEEPSAKE
1976

Recto: facsimile of Fitzgerald's holograph notes for proposed Ring Lardner collection; verso: menu of Hotel Chatham, 11 December 1923.

Colophon: '300 copies printed to mark publication of *Ring Lardner: A Descriptive Bibliography* by Matthew J. Bruccoli and Richard Layman. . . .'

Columbia, S.C.: Bruccoli & Layman, 1976.

Single pale orange-yellow (#73) sheet printed on both sides. 7$^{1}/_{16}$″ × 10$^{13}/_{16}$″ .

Locations: Lilly; MJB; PSt.

Reproduced in Jonathan Yardley, *Ring* (New York: Random House, [1977]), following p. 274.

H 12 LETTER KEEPSAKE
1978

Facsimile of Fitzgerald's letter to Maxwell Perkins, fall 1924: 'The royalty was better than I'd expected. This is to tell you about a young man named Ernest Hemmingway. . . .'

Colophon: 'Five Hundred Copies Printed To Mark Publication of SCOTT AND ERNEST By Matthew J. Bruccoli (New York: Random House, 1978).'

Columbia, S.C.: Bruccoli, 1978.

Single yellow white (#92) sheet printed on both sides. 8$^{1}/_{2}$″ × 10$^{15}/_{16}$″.

Locations: Lilly; MJB; NjP; PSt.

H 13 LIBRARY CARD KEEPSAKE
1978

Recto: facsimile of Fitzgerald's library card for the Louisville Free Public Library, 1918; verso: 9 entries from Fitzgerald's *Notebooks,* of which 6 were previously unpublished.

New York: Harcourt Brace Jovanovich / Bruccoli Clark, 1978.

Single light yellow-brown (#76) sheet printed on both sides. 5″ × 7″.

2,000 copies distributed to mark publication of *The Notebooks of F. Scott Fitzgerald.*

Locations: Lilly; MJB: NjP; PSt.

I. Zelda Fitzgerald's Publications

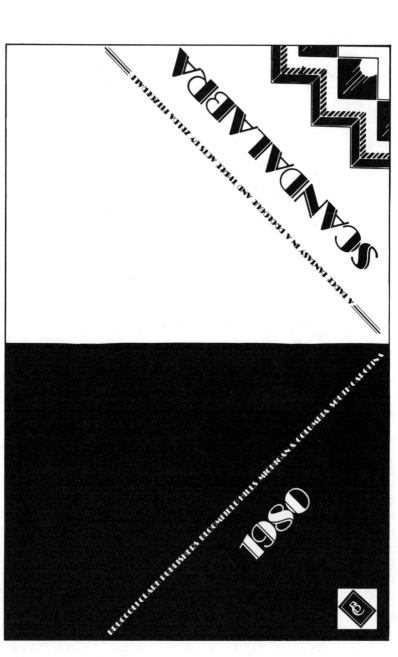

I 3 *(p. 305)*

Note: Reprinted by the Book-of-the-Month Club in 1972. These copies have an altered copyright page and omit the card page; bound in black cloth with blind-stamped square on back cover.

I 13 *(p. 306)*
"What Became of the Flappers?" *McCall's,* LIII (October 1925), 12, 30, 66.

Published with Fitzgerald's "Our Young Rich Boys" under the joint title "What Becomes of Our Flappers and Sheiks?"

Article. See C 156‡.

I 25 *(p. 308)*
Fiction.

I 30 *(p. 309)*
Note: Offset piracy of *Zelda* probably printed in Taiwan.

I 32
"The Fitzgerald Flappers," *St. Paul Daily News* (11 April 1926), III, 6.

Interview.

I 33

[3 flowers and swan] | [on ribbon] PARFOIS LA FOLIE EST LA SAGESSE | [below ribbon] PAINTINGS | by | ZELDA FITZGERALD | PHOTOGRAPHS | by | MARION HINES | March 29–April 30–1934 | 525 EAST 86th Street | NEW YORK, N.Y.

Folio. Exhibition catalogue. Does not include text by ZF. Reproduced in *Fitzgerald/ Hemingway Annual 1972,* pp. 36–37, and *The Romantic Egoists,* p. 195.

I 34
Bits of Paradise. London: Bodley Head, [1973].

Includes 10 stories by Zelda Fitzgerald. See A 39‡.

I 35
The Romantic Egoists. New York: Scribners, [1974].

Reproduces paintings and quotes from writings throughout. See B 94‡.

I 36

[silver, decorated with flowers] Zelda | [black] Zelda Sayre Fitzgerald Retrospective

[Montgomery: Montgomery Museum of Fine Arts, 1974].

Wrappers. Exhibition catalogue, with reproductions of paintings.

I 37

"Zelda Fitzgerald's Tribute to F. Scott Fitzgerald," *Fitzgerald/Hemingway Annual 1974*, pp. 2–7.

I 38

Littleton, Taylor. "A Letter from Zelda Fitzgerald," *Fitzgerald/Hemingway Annual 1975*, pp. 3–6.

SCANDALABRA

I 39
First edition, only printing

On copyright page: 'Copyright © 1980 by Scottie Fitzgerald Smith'.

Certificate of limitation: 'This First Edition of *Scandalabra* | is Limited to 500 Numbered Copies. | Copies 1 to 450 Are for Sale; | Copies I to L Are Reserved | for the Publisher. This is copy | [thick and thin rules]'.

[1–64]

[1]^{32}

Contents: p. 1: front cover; pp. 2–3: title; p. 4: copyright; p. 5: certificate of limitation and colophon; p. 6: facsimile of program; pp. 7–8: 'Foreward' by Meredith Walker; pp. 9–62: text, headed 'PROLOGUE'; p. 63: 'Editorial Note'; p. 64: back cover.

Typography and paper: 7⅝″ × 5⁵⁄₁₆″ (ragged right); rules at right and bottom margins with art deco design at lower right corner of recto pages. Warren's Olde Style wove cream white paper.

Binding: 64-page booklet inserted in pocket of portfolio. Portfolio: 11½″ × 9″; black paper-covered boards with black cloth shelfback; facsimile of Zelda Fitzgerald's signature in white on front; lined with light purple paper; light green triangular pocket. Booklet: 10⁷⁄₁₆″ × 7¹⁵⁄₁₆″; front cover has art deco design in white on black; solid black back cover.

Publication: Published 15 April 1980. See note following I 31.

Printing: Composed by BC Research, Columbia, S.C. Printed by the Wickersham Printing Co., Lancaster, Pa. Bound by A. Horowitz & Sons, Fairfield, N.J. Designed by Barbara DuPree Knowles; Peter H. Grant, production supervisor.

Locations: LC; MJB; Princeton.

Note: See Matthew J. Bruccoli, "Zelda Fitzgerald's Lost Stories," *Fitzgerald/Hemingway Annual 1979* for synopses of 8 unpublished stories.

J. Translations

Translations of a particular work by Fitzgerald are listed by language. Languages are alphabetical under Fitzgerald's titles, which are chronological.

THIS SIDE OF PARADISE

BENGALI

J1
[This Side of Paradise], trans. Sanaullah Nuri. Dacca, Pakistan: M/S Book Villa, 1970.

CZECH

J2
NA PRAHU RÄJE, trans. Josef Hochman. Prague: Libuše Vrbová, 1971.

DUTCH

J3
DEZE KANT VAN HET PARADIJS, trans. Clara Eggink and Omslagontwerp van Uniepers. Amsterdam: Contact, 1971.

FRENCH

J4
L'ENVERS DU PARADIS, trans. Suzanne Mayoux. Paris: Gallimard, 1964.

ITALIAN

J5
DI QUA DAL PARADISO, trans. Fernanda Pivano. Milan and Verona: Mondadori, 1952. Reprinted 1961, 1964, 1968, 1969.

No attempt has been made in this section to follow the systems for printing titles in the languages represented; all foreign-language book titles are set in italic capitals. Not all of the translations listed here have been examined by the compiler: some are from *Index Translationum* (Paris: UNESCO, 1950). Most of these entries are drawn from Linda Berry and Patricia Powell, "Fitzgerald in Translation," *Fitzgerald/Hemingway Annual 1972,* and Linda Berry, "Fitzgerald in Translation II," *Fitzgerald/Hemingway Annual 1974.*

JAPANESE

J6
RAKUEN NO KOCHIRAGAWA, trans. Katsuji Takamura. Tokyo: Areci Shuppan-sha, 1957.

KOREAN

J7
NAGWEONEUI IJJOG, trans. Yang Byeong Tag. Seoul: Eulyu, 1969.

PORTUGUESE

J8
ÊSTE LADO DO PARAÍSO, trans. Brenno Silveira. Rio de Janeiro: Editôra Civilização Brasileira, 1962. Reprinted 1965.

SERBO-CROATIAN

J9
S OVE STRANE RAJA, trans. Ljerka Radovíc. Belgrade: Narodna knjiga, 1964.

SPANISH

J10
A ESTE LADO DEL PARAÍSO, trans. Juan Benet Goitia. Madrid: Alianza Editorial, 1968.

THE BEAUTIFUL AND DAMNED

FINNISH

J11
KAUNIS JA KADOTUKSEEN TUOMITTU, trans. Antero Hälvä. Helsinki: Otava, 1954.

FRENCH

J12
LES HEUREUX ET LES DAMNÉS, trans. Louise Servicen. Paris: Gallimard, 1964.

ITALIAN

J13
BELLI E DANNATI, trans. Fernanda Pivano. Milan and Verona: Mondadori, 1954.

J 14
BELOS E MALDITOS, trans. Waltensir Dutra. Rio de Janeiro: Editôra Civilização Brasileira, 1963. Reprinted 1965.

J 15
BELOS E MALDITOS, trans. H. Silva Letra. Lisbon: Portugália, 1968.

SERBO-CROATIAN

J 16
LEPI I PROKLETI, trans. Dušanka Todorović. Novi Sad, Yugoslavia: Bratstvo-Jedinstvo, 1969.

SPANISH

J 17
[The Beautiful and Damned, translator undetermined]. Santiago, Chile: Zig-Zag, 1970.

THE VEGETABLE

DUTCH

J 18
VEGETEREN, trans. Ernest van Altena. Amsterdam: Contact, 1974.

FRENCH

J 19
LE LEGUME, trans. Jean Loup Dabodie. Paris: Laffont, 1972.

ITALIAN

J 20
POSTINO O PRESIDENTE? trans. Domenico Tarizzo. Milan: Il Saggiatore, 1962.

THE GREAT GATSBY

ARABIC

J 21
[The Great Gatsby], trans. Najeeb Al Mania. Baghdad: Haider Al Jawady, 1962.

BENGALI

J 22
[The Great Gatsby], trans. Kabir Chowdhury. Pakistan: M/S Bright Book House, 1971.

BULGARIAN

J 23
VELIKIJAT GETSBI, trans. Neli Dospevska. Sofia, Bulgaria: Nar. Kultura, 1966.

CATALAN

J 24
EL GRAN GATSBY, trans. Ramón Folch i Camarasa. Barcelona: Edicions 62, 1967.

CHINESE

J 25
YUNG HÊNG CHIH LÜAN, trans. Huang Shu-Shen. Taipei: Cheng Chung Book Co., 1954.

J 26
TA TSAI! KAI SHIH PI, trans. Wang Jun Hua and T'an Ying. Tainan: Chung Hua Pub. Ser., 1969.

J 27
[The Great Gatsby], trans. George Kao. Hong Kong: World Today Press, 1971.

CZECH

J 28
VELKÝ GATSBY, trans. Lubomír Dorůžka. Prague: SNKLHU, 1960.

DANISH

J 29
DEN STORE GATSBY, trans. Ove Brusendorff. Copenhagen: Thaning & Appel, 1948. Reprinted: Copenhagen: Gyldendal, 1960, 1971 (wrappers); Copenhagen: Gyldendals Bogklub, 1971 (cloth).

DUTCH

J 30
DE GROTE GATSBY, trans. L. Cornils. Amsterdam: G. A. van Oorschot, 1948. Reprinted: Amsterdam: Contact, 1968, 1973.

ESTONIAN

J31
SUUR GATSBY, trans. Enn Soosaar. Tallinn, USSR: Ëêsti raamat, 1966.

FINNISH

J32   *KULTAHATTU,* [translator undetermined]. Helsinki: Otava, 1959.

FRENCH

J33
GATSBY LE MAGNIFIQUE, trans. Victor Llona. Paris: Collection Européene, Kra Edit,
1926. Reprinted: Paris: Sagittaire, 1946; Paris: le Club français du livre, 1952, 1959;
Paris: Grasset, 1962, 1968; Paris: Livre de poche, 1962; Paris: Editions Rombaldi,
1969; Paris: le Club de la femme, 1969.

GERMAN

J34
DER GROSSE GATSBY, trans. M. Lazar. Berlin: Knaur, 1928. Reprinted 1932.

J35
DER GROSSE GATSBY, trans. Walter Schürenberg. Berlin: Blanvalet, 1953. Reprinted:
Frankfurt: Büchergilde Gutenberg, 1958; Berlin and Weimar: Aufbau-Verlag, 1968.

GREEK

J36
GOTSBY O MAGHAS, trans. Manthos Crispis. Athens: Oi filoi tis Loghotechnias, 1955.

HEBREW

J37
GATSBY HAGADOL, trans. Menahem Ben-Asher. Tel Aviv: Mazpen, 1962.

J38
GATSBY HA-GADOL, trans. Gideon Toury. Tel Aviv: Sifre Siman Kri'a, Mif'alim Univer-
sita'iyim le-Hoza'a La'or, 1974.

HINDI

J39
LALASA, trans. Ajeya. Delhi, India: Rajpal, 1969.

J40
A NAGY GATSBY, trans. Elek Máthé. Budapest: Szépirodalmi Könyvkiado, 1953.

J41
URJA BABILONBAN, trans. Elek Máthé. Budapest: Magvetö, 1962. With stories and other writings by Fitzgerald.

ITALIAN

J42
IL GRANDE GATSBY, trans. Fernanda Pivano. Milan and Verona: Mondadori, 1950. Reprinted 1958, 1961, 1964, 1965.

JAPANESE

J43
IDAINARU GATSBY, trans. Takashi Nozaki. Tokyo: Kenkyû-sha, 1957. With stories by Fitzgerald.

J44
YUME AWAKI SEISHUN, trans. Saburô Ônuki. Tokyo: Kadokawa Shoten, 1957.

KOREAN

J45
WI'DAE'HAN GATSBY, trans. Gweon Eung-ho. Seoul: Sin'yang'sa, 1959.

LITHUANIAN

J46
DIDYSIS GETSBIS, trans. G. Zolubiene. Vilnius, USSR: Vaga, 1967.

MACEDONIAN

J47
GOLEMIOT GEJTZBI, trans. Vera Jančevska. Skopje, Yugoslavia: Kočo Racin, 1965.

NORWEGIAN

J48
DEN GULE BIL, trans. T. Thomsen. Oslo: Gyldendal, 1927.

J49
DEN STORE GATSBY, trans. Peter Magus. Oslo: Gyldendal Norsk Forlag, 1951. Reprinted 1965.

PERSIAN

J50
[The Great Gatsby], trans. Karim Emami. Teheran: Sherkat Saroid, 1966.

POLISH

J51
WIELKI GATSBY, trans. Ariadna Demkowska. Warsaw: Czytelnik, 1962. Reprinted 1964, 1973.

PORTUGUESE

J52
O GRANDE GATSBY, trans. J. R. Miguéis. Lisbon: Portugália, 1960. Reprinted 1962.

J53
O GRANDE GATSBY, trans. Brenno Silveira. Rio de Janeiro: Civilização Brasileira, 1962, 1965. Reprinted: São Paulo: Círculo do Livro, 1977.

ROMANIAN

J54
MARELE GATSBY, trans. Mircea Ivănescu. Bucharest: Editura pentru literatură universală, 1967.

RUSSIAN

J55
VELIKIJ GĔTSBI, trans. E. Kalašnikova. Moscow: Hudož, 1966.

SERBO-CROATIAN

J56
SNAGA LJUBAVI, trans. Jovan Vagenhals. Sarajevo: Džepna knjiga, 1956.

J57
VELIKI GATSBY, trans. Šime Balen. Zagreb, Yugoslavia: Zora, 1959.

J58
VELIKI GETSBI, trans. Saša Petrović. Belgrade: "Rad," 1964. Reprinted 1968.

J59
VELIKI GETSBI I ČETIRI PRIČE, trans. Saša Petrović and Dragoslav Andrić. Belgrade: Yugoslavia, 1967. With stories by Fitzgerald.

SLOVAK

J 60
VEL'KY GATSBY, [translator undetermined]. Bratislava: Slovensky Spisovatel, 1970.

SLOVENE

J 61
VELIK GATSBY, trans. Gitica Jakopinov. Ljubljana, Yugoslavia: Mladinska knjiga, 1961.
Reprinted: Cankarjeva založba, 1970.

SPANISH

J 62
EL GRAN GATSBY, trans. Armando Alvarez Bravo. Havana: Editorial Nacional de
Cuba, 1965.

J 63
EL GRAN GATSBY, trans. E. Piñas. Barcelona: Plaza & Janes, 1970. Reprinted Guada-
lupe and Barcelona: Plaza y Janes, 1975.

SWEDISH

J 64
EN MAN UTAN SKRUPLER, trans. Siri Thorngren-Olin. Stockholm: Wahlström & Widstrand, 1928.

J 65.
DEN STORE GATSBY, trans. Gösta Olzon. Stockholm: Bonnier, 1946. Reprinted 1955,
1963.

J 66
[The Great Gatsby], trans. Ulla Britta Halden. Stockholm: Polyglot Club [Seelig], 1950.
See A 11.9.

TURKISH

J 67
MUHTEŞM GATSBY, trans. Can Yücel. Istanbul: Ağaoğlu Yayinevi, 1964.

TENDER IS THE NIGHT

AFRIKAANS

J 68
TEER IS DIE NAG, trans. Jan Vorster. Johannesburg: Boek Mosaiek, 1968.

BULGARIAN

J 69
NEŽNA E NOŠTTA, trans. Dimitri Ivanov. Sofia, Bulgaria: Nar. Kultura, 1967.

CATALAN

J 70
TENDRA E LA NIT, trans. Ramón Terenci Moix. Barcelona: Edicions 62, 1968.

CZECH

J 71
NĚŽNÁ JE NOC, trans. Lubomír Dorůžka. Prague: Odeon, 1968.

DANISH

J 72
NATTEN ER BLID, trans. Helga Vang Lauridsen and Elsa Gress. Copenhagen: Wangel, 1954. Reprinted: Copenhagen: Skrifola, 1961; Copenhagen: Gyldendal, 1972.

DUTCH

J 73
TEDER IS DE NACHT, trans. H. W. J. Schaap. Amsterdam: Contact, 1969.

FINNISH

J 74
YÖ ON HELLÄ, [translator undetermined]. Helsinki: Werner Söderstrom Osakeyhtiö, 1975.

FRENCH

J 75
TENDRE EST LA NUIT, trans. Marguerite Chevalley. Paris: Stock, 1951. Reprinted: Paris: Delamain et Boutelleau, 1951; Brussels: Les Editions Biblis, 1953; Lausanne: Ed. Rencontre, 1965; Paris: Stock, 1967; Paris: Livre de poche, 1969.

GERMAN

J 76
ZÄRTLICH IST DIE NACHT, trans. Grete Rambach. Berlin: Blanvalet, 1952. Reprinted 1968; Berlin: Aufbau-Verlag, 1976.

GREEK

J 77
TRYPHERI EINAI E NYKTA, trans. Mina Zographou. Athens: Galaxias, 1961.

HUNGARIAN

J 78
AZ ÉJ SZELÍD TRÓNJÁN, trans. Osztovits Levente. Budapest: Európa Könyvkiadó, 1972.

ITALIAN

J 79
TENERA È LA NOTTE, trans. Fernanda Pivano. Turin: Einaudi, 1949. Reprinted 1957; Milan and Verona: Mondadori, 1958; Milan: Mondadori, 1967, 1972.

JAPANESE

J 80
YORU WA YASASHI, trans. Rikuo Tangiguchi. Tokyo: Kadokawa Shoten, 1960.

POLISH

J 81
CZUTA JEST NOC, trans. Maria Skroczynska and Zofia Zinserling. Warsaw: Czytelnik, 1967.

PORTUGUESE

J 82
TERNA É A NOITE, trans. Cabral do Nascimento. Lisbon: Portugália, 1962.

J 83
SUAVE É A NOITE, trans. Lígia Junqueira. Rio de Janeiro: Civilização Brasileira, 1964. Reprinted: São Paulo: Círculo do Livro, 1976.

SERBO-CROATIAN

J 84
BLAGA JE NÓC, trans. Bora Glišić. Subotica, Yugoslavia: Minerva, 1956. Reprinted 1958.

SLOVAK

J 85
NEŽNÁ JE NOC, trans. Tatjana Ruppeldtová. Bratislava, Czechoslovakia: SVKL, 1965.

SLOVENE

J86
NEŽNA JE NOČ, trans. Aljoša Furlan. Ljubljana, Yugoslavia: Cankarjeva založba, 1967.

SPANISH

J87
SUAVE ES LA NOCHE, trans. Marcelo Cervelló. Barcelona: Plaza y Janés, 1963. Reprinted 1972.

SWEDISH

J88
NATTEN ÄR LJUV, trans. Arna Hägglund. Stockholm: Wahlström & Widstrand, 1952.

TURKISH

J89
GECELER GÜZELDIR, trans. Azize Erten Bergin. Istanbul: Tifdruk Matbaacilik Sanayii A. Ş. Marbaasi, 1962. Reprinted Istanbul: Altin Kitaplar Yayinevi, 1973.

J90
YABANCIYA GÖNÜL VERME, trans. Semih Yazicioglu. Istanbul: Celikcilt Matbaasi, 1962.

THE LAST TYCOON

DUTCH

J91
DE LAATSTE FILMMAGNAAT, trans. Ernest van Altena. Amsterdam: Contact, 1975.

FRENCH

J92
LE DERNIER NABAB, trans. André Michel. Paris: Gallimard, 1952.

J93
LE DERNIER NABAB, trans. Suzanne Mayoux. France: Gallimard, 1976.

GERMAN

J94
DER LETZTE TAIKUN, trans. Walter Schürenberg. Frankfurt: Suhrkamp, 1962. Reprinted: Zurich: Diogenes, 1977.

ITALIAN

J 95
GLI ULTIMI FUOCHI, trans. Bruno Oddera. Milan and Verona: Mondadori, 1959. Reprinted 1962, 1968, 1974; Milan: Mondadori, 1977.

PORTUGUESE

J 96
O ULTIMO MAGNATA, trans. Roberto Pontual. Rio de Janeiro: Editôra Civilização Brasileira, 1967. Reprinted: Rio de Janeiro: Record, [1977].

SPANISH

J 97
EL ÚLTIMO MAGNATE, trans. Cecelia Boissier and Antonio Skarmeta. Santiago, Chile: Zig-Zag; Madrid: Rodas, 1972. Reprinted: Rodas, 1975.

SWEDISH

J 98
DEN SISTE MAGNATEN, trans. Gunnar Barkland. Stockholm: Wahlström & Widstrand, 1975.

THE CRACK-UP

ITALIAN

J 99
L'ETÀ DEL JAZZ E ALTRI SCRITTI, trans. Domenico Tarizzo. Milan: Il Saggiatore, 1960. Reprinted: Milan: Club degli editori, 1963; Milan: Il Saggiatore, 1966.

PORTUGUESE

J 100
A DERROCADA E OUTROS CONTOS E TEXTOS AUTOBIOGRÁFICOS, trans. Alvaro Cabral. Rio de Janeiro: Civilização Brasileira, 1969.

SPANISH

J 101
EL DERRUMBE, [translator undetermined]. Santiago, Chile: Zig-Zag, 1970.

SWEDISH

J 102
SAMMANBROTTET, trans. Olle Carlsson and Sven Hamrell. Stockholm: Rabén and Sjögren, 1957. Reprinted 1964.

AFTERNOON OF AN AUTHOR

DANISH

J 103
EN FORFATTERS EFTERMIDDAG, trans. Hans Hertel. Copenhagen: Hasselbalch, 1967.

ITALIAN

J 104
CREPUSCOLO DI UNO SCRITTORE, trans. Giorgio Monicelli. Milan: Mondadori, 1966.

POLISH

J 105
HISTORIA JEDNEGO WYJAZDU, trans. Agnieszka Glinczanka. Warsaw: Pánstw. Instytut Wydawn, 1963.

THE PAT HOBBY STORIES

DUTCH

J 106
PAT HOBBY AAN LAGER WAL IN HOLLYWOOD, trans. Guido Golüke. Amsterdam: Contact, 1977.

FRENCH

J 107
HISTOIRES DE PAT HOBBY ET AUTRES NOUVELLES, trans. Marie-Pierre Castelnau and Bernard Willerval. Paris: Laffont, 1965.

SPANISH

J 108
HISTORIAS DE PAT HOBBY, trans. Alberto Luis Pérez. Barcelona: Luis de Caralt, 1970.

THE LETTERS OF F. SCOTT FITZGERALD

FRENCH

J 109
LETTRES DE F. SCOTT FITZGERALD, ed. Andrew Turnbull; trans. J. and L. Bréant. Paris: Gallimard, 1966.

SHORT STORIES

ARABIC

J 110
["Babylon Revisited"], trans. Abbas Mahmoud el-Akkad. In [*Facets of the Short Story (Novellette) in American Literature*]. Cairo: Dar Akhbas el-Youm, 1954.

BENGALI

J 111
PANCHAMUKKI, trans. Atwar Rahman. Dacca, Pakistan: Popular Publications, 1962.

CHINESE

J 112
TUNG JIH MÊNG, trans. Huang Ching Hsi. Hong Kong: World Today Press, 1963.

CZECH

J 113
DIAMANT VELKÝ JAKO RITZ, trans. Zdeněk Urbánek and Lubomír Dorůžka. Prague: SNKLU, 1964. Reprinted 1965.

DANISH

J 114
"DEN RIGE DRENG," trans. H. Lassen. In *UDENFOR SAESONEN OG ANDRE AMERI-KANSKE NOVELLER,* ed. S. M. Kristensen. Copenhagen: C. Andersen Forlag, 1956.

J 115
TILBAGE TIL BABYLON, trans. Bendix Bech-Thostrup and Elise Norsbo. Copenhagen: Carit Andersen, 1966.

J 116
HISTORIER FRA JAZZTIDEN, trans. Hans Hertel. Copenhagen: Hasselbalch, 1967.

DUTCH

J 117
EEN ALKOHOLISCH GEVAL EN ANDERE VERHALEN, trans. Jean A. Schalekamp. Amsterdam: Contact, 1971.

J 118
VERHALEN UIT DE TIJD VAN DE JAZZ, trans. Jean A. Schalekamp. Amsterdam: Contact, 1971.

J 119
GEKKE ZONDAG EN ANDERE VERHALEN, trans. Jean A. Schalekamp. Amsterdam: Contact, 1972.

J 120
DE DIAMANT DIE ZO GROOT WAS ALS DE RITZ, trans. Jan Donkers. Amsterdam: Contact, 1977.

FRENCH

J 121
LA FÊLURE, trans. Dominique Aury and Suzanne Mayoux. Paris: Gallimard, 1963.

J 122
UN DIAMANT GROS COMME LE RITZ, trans. Marie-Pierre Castelnau and Bernard Willerval. Paris: Laffont, 1964.

J 123
LA LONGUE FUITE, trans. Marie-Pierre Castelnau and Bernard Willerval. Lausanne: La Guilde du livre, 1964.

J 124
LES ENFANTS DU JAZZ, trans. Suzanne Mayoux. Paris: Gallimard, 1967.

J 125
F. S. Fitzgerald/Short Stories/Nouvelles, ed. Andre Le Vot, trans. Marie-Pierre Castlenau and Bernard Willerval. Paris: Aubier-Flammarion, 1972. Contains "Absolution," "May Day," "Babylon Revisited." Bilingual text.

J 126
ECLATS DU PARADIS, trans. Jean Queval. Paris: Julliard, 1977.

GERMAN

J 127
DIE BESTEN STORIES, trans. Walter Schürenberg. Berlin: Blanvalet, 1954.

J 128
AUS DEN TOLLEN ZWANZIGER JAHREN, trans. Theo Schumacher. Ebenhausen b. München: Langewiesche-Brandt, 1963.

J 129
EIN DIAMANT, SO GROß WIE DAS RITZ, trans. Elga Abramowitz and Walter Schürenberg. Berlin: Aufbau-Verlag, 1972.

HUNGARIAN

J 130
AZ ÓLOMKRISTÁLY ÉS EGYÉB ÍRÁSOK, trans. Béla Abody, Antal Árkos et al. Budapest: Európa Könyvkiadó, 1966.

INDONESIAN

J 131
ORANG KAJA, [translator undetermined]. Jakarta: Balai Pustaka, 1950.

ITALIAN

J 132
BASIL E CLEOPATRA, trans. Domenico Tarizzo and Cesare Salmaggi. Milan: Il Saggiatore, 1960.

J 133
L'ETÀ DEL JAZZ, trans. Domenico Tarizzo. Milan: Il Saggiatore, 1960.

J 134
28 RACCONTI, trans. Bruno Oddera. Milan: Mondadori, 1960.

J 135
L'ETÀ DEL JAZZ E ALTRI SCRITTI, trans. Domenico Tarizzo. New ed. Milan: Il Saggiatore, 1966.

J 136
RACCONTI DELL'ETÀ DEL JAZZ, trans. Giorgio Monicelli and Bruno Oddera. Milan: Mondadori, 1968.

J 137
IL DIAMANTE GROSSO COME L'HOTEL RITZ, trans, Burno Oddera. Milan: Mondadori, 1974.

J 138
LEMBI DI PARADISO, trans. V. Mantovani and B. Oddera. Verona: Mondadori, [1975].

J 139
I RACCONTE DI BASIL E JOSEPHINE, trans. Giulia Fretta, Giorgio Monicelli, and Bruno Oddera. Verona: Mondadori, 1976.

JAPANESE

J 140
AME NO ASA PARIS NI SHISU, trans. Kô Shimuzu. Tokyo: Mikasa shobô, 1955.

J141
AME NO ASA PARIS NI SHISU, trans. Yoshide Iijima. Tokyo: Kadokawa Shoten, 1955; rev. ed. 1968.

J142
FUYU NO YUME, trans. Kazuyo Nishi and Sakae Morioka. Tokyo: Eihô-sha, 1956.

J143
["Babylon Revisited," "The Cut-Glass Bowl," "Absolution"], trans. Junshu Jijima. Tokyo: Kadokawa Shoten, 1957.

J144
YÛFUKUNA SEINEN, trans. Yôkichi Miyamoto and Reijmi Nagakawa. Tokyo: Nan'un-dô, 1958.

NORWEGIAN

J145
NOVELLER, trans. Gordon Holmebakk. Oslo: Gyldendal, 1965.

J146
NOVELLER, trans. Helge Hagerup. Oslo: Gyldendal, 1965.

POLISH

J147
ODWIEDZINY W BABILONIE, trans. Adam Kaska. Warsaw: Czytelnik, 1963. Reprinted: Warsaw: Ksiazka i Wiedza, 1967.

PORTUGUESE

J148
SEIS CONTOS DE ERA DO JAZZ, trans. Brenno Silveira. Rio de Janeiro: Editôra Civilização Brasileira, 1962. Reprinted 1965.

RUSSIAN

J149
VOZVRAŠČENIE V VAVILON, trans. Ekaterina Vasil'eva. Moscow: Pravda, 1969.

SERBO-CROATIAN

J150
PONOVO U VAVILONU, trans. Dragoslav Andrić. Belgrade: Omladina, 1958.

SPANISH

J151
JOVENCITAS Y FILÓSOFOS, trans. Oscar Luis Molina. Barcelona: Caralt, 1969.

J 152
LOS RELATOS DE BASIL Y JOSEPHINE, trans. Rafael Ruiz de la Cuesta. Madrid:
Alianza, 1977.

TURKISH

J 153
1 MAYIS, trans. R. Tomris Uyar. Istanbul: Gerçek Yayinevi, 1968.

COLLECTED WORKS

ITALIAN

J 154
ROMANZI, trans. Fernanda Pivano and Domenico Tarizzo. Milan and Verona: Monda-
dori, 1972. Contains *This Side of Paradise, The Beautiful and Damned, The Great
Gatsby, Tender Is the Night,* and *The Crack-Up.*

JAPANESE

J 155
[This Side of Paradise, Tender Is the Night, Short Stories] ("Babylon Revisited," "Family
in the Wind," "Winter Dreams"), trans. Katsuji Takamura. In *[Collection of Contemporary American Literature].* Vol. 3. Tokyo: Arachi, 1957.

ZELDA FITZGERALD'S SAVE ME THE WALTZ

FRENCH

J 156
ACCORDEZ-MOI CETTE VALSE, trans. Jacqueline Remillet. Paris: Laffont, 1973.

GERMAN

J 157
DARF ICH UM DEN WALZER BITTEN? trans. Elizabeth Schnack. Olten: Walter-Verlag,
1972.

K. Republications

This section lists anthology, magazine, and newspaper republications in the English language of Fitzgerald's stories, poems, essays, interviews, and excerpts from novels—all writings except letters. An entry that has not been examined by the compiler is identified with an asterisk.

Many of these items are drawn from Margaret M. Duggan's "Reprintings of Fitzgerald," *Fitzgerald/Hemingway Annual 1974.* Others are based on the *Cumulative Book Index* and the *National Union Catalog.* Although this list is certainly incomplete, it provides a gauge of the visibility of Fitzgerald's work and the popularity of particular pieces.

Fitzgerald's works are alphabetical. Republications of each work are listed chronologically.

"ABSOLUTION" (STORY)

K 1
Studies in the Short Story, ed. Adrian H. Jaffe and Virgil Scott. New York: Holt, Rinehart & Winston, 1960*; rev. ed., 1966, 1968.

K 2
A College Book of Modern Fiction, ed. Walter B. Rideout and James K. Robinson. Evanston & Elmsford: Row, Peterson, 1961.

K 3*
Introduction to Literature: Stories, ed. Lynn Altenbernd and Leslie L. Lewis. New York: Macmillan, 1963, 1969.

K 4
The Dimensions of the Short Story, ed. James E. Miller, Jr., and Bernice Slote. New York & Toronto: Dodd, Mead, 1964.

K 5*
Twelve Short Stories, ed. Marvin Magalaner and Edmond L. Volpe. 2nd series. New York: Macmillan, 1969. (First series not seen.)

K 5a
Fitzgerald's The Great Gatsby, ed. Henry Dan Piper. New York: Scribners, 1970.

K 6*
Youth and Maturity: 20 Short Stories, ed. James S. Coulos. New York: Macmillan, 1970.

K 7*
Vision and Value   A Thematic Introduction to the Short Story, ed. James Nagel. Belmont, Calif.: Dickenson, 1970.

K 8*
Fiction 100, ed. James H. Pickering. New York: Macmillan, 1974.

"Winter Dreams" was substituted for this story in the 1978 edition. See K 397‡.

K 9*
Studies in the Short Story, ed. Virgil Scott and David Madden. New York: Holt, Rinehart & Winston, 1976.

149

"THE ADJUSTER" (STORY)

K 10*
A Lady's Pleasure, ed. J. L. Collins. New York: Penn, 1946.

CONTRIBUTIONS TO *THE NEW AMERICAN CREDO*

K 11
The New American Credo, ed. George Jean Nathan. New York: Knopf, 1927.
See B 82‡.

"AT YOUR AGE" (STORY)

K 12
Great Modern Short Stories, ed. Grant Overton. New York: Modern Library, 1930.
See B 12.

K 13
Husbands and Lovers, ed. Joseph Greene and Elizabeth Abell. New York: Bantam, 1949.

"BABYLON REVISITED" (STORY)

K 14
The Best Short Stories of 1931, Vol. II (American), ed. Edward J. O'Brien. New York: Dodd, Mead, 1931; London: Cape, 1932.

See B 13.

K 15*
A Quarto of Modern Literature, ed. Leonard S. Brown and Porter G. Perrin. New York: Scribners, 1935, 1940.

"The Rich Boy" was substituted for this story in the third edition of 1950. See K 307‡.

K 16*
A Study of the Short Story, ed. Henry Seidel Canby and Alfred S. Dashiell. New York: Holt, 1935.

K 17
50 Best American Short Stories 1915–1939, ed. Edward J. O'Brien. Boston: Houghton Mifflin, 1939; New York: Literary Guild of America, 1939*.

K 18
Present-Day Stories, ed. John T. Frederick. New York: Scribners, 1941.

K 19*
Great Modern Reading, ed. W. Somerset Maugham. Garden City: N.Y.: Doubleday: 1943.

Reprinted as *W. Somerset Maugham's Introduction to Modern English and American Literature*. New York: New Home Library, 1943; Philadelphia: Blakiston, 1943.

K 20
The Pocket Book of Modern American Short Stories, ed. Philip Van Doren Stern. Philadelphia: Blakiston, 1943*; New York: Pocket Books, 1943; New York: Washington Square, 1953.

K 21*
A Treasury of Short Stories, ed. Bernadine Kielty. New York: Simon & Schuster, 1947.

K 22
The College Short Story Reader, ed. Harry W. Hastings. New York: Odyssey Press, 1948.

K 23
Introduction to Literature, ed. L. G. Locke, W. M. Gibson, and George Arms. New York: Rinehart, 1948.

K 24*
Readings for a Liberal Education, ed. L. G. Locke, W. M. Gibson, and George W. Arms. New York: Rinehart, 1948.

K 25
American Literature   An Anthology and Critical Survey, ed. Joe Lee Davis, John T. Frederick, and Frank Luther Mott. New York: Scribners, 1949.

K 26
The Critical Reader, ed. Wallace Douglas, Roy Lamson, and Hallett Smith. New York: Norton, 1949.

K 27
The College Miscellany, ed. Samuel N. Bogorad and Jack Trevithick. New York: Rinehart, 1952.

K 28
Short Stories in Context, ed. Woodburn O. Ross and A. Dayle Wallace. New York: American Book Co., 1953.

K 29*
Stories: British and American, ed. J. B. Ludwig and W. R. Poirier. Boston: Houghton Mifflin, 1953.

K 30
Contemporary Short Stories   Representative Selections, Vol. II, ed. Maurice Baudin, Jr. Indianapolis & New York: Bobbs-Merrill, 1954*; New York: Liberal Arts Press, 1954.

K 31
The Saturday Evening Post Treasury, ed. Roger Butterfield. New York: Simon & Schuster, 1954.

K 32*
A Treasury of American Literature, Vol. II, ed. Joe Lee Davis, John T. Frederick, and Frank Luther Mott. Chicago: Spencer, 1955.

K 33
American Stories; Isolated People in the Modern World, Vol. VI, ed. Theodor Wolpers. Paderborn: Verlag Ferdinand Schöningh, 1956.

K 34
The American Tradition in Literature, Vol. II, ed. Sculley Bradley, Richmond Croom Beatty, and E. Hudson Long. New York: Norton, 1956*, 1957*, 1961*, 1962*, 1967, 1974*.

K 35
A College Treasury, Vol. II, ed. Paul A. Jorgensen and Frederick B. Shroyer. New York: Scribners, 1956, 1967.

K 36
A College Treasury, Prose, Fiction, Drama, Poetry, ed. Paul A. Jorgensen and Frederick B. Shroyer. New York: Scribners, 1956, 1967.

K 37*
The Growth of American Literature   A Critical and Historical Survey, Vol. II, ed. Edwin Harrison Cady, Frederick J. Hoffman, and Roy Harvey Pearce. New York: American Book Co., 1956.

K 38
American Poetry and Prose, Vol. II, ed. Norman Foerster. 4th ed. Boston: Houghton Mifflin, 1957. (Earlier editions not seen.)

K 39
More Stories to Remember, Vol. II, ed. Thomas B. Costain and John Beecroft. Garden City, N.Y.: Doubleday, 1958; Vol. IV, New York: Popular Library, 1958.

K 40
Short Fiction: A Critical Collection, ed. James R. Frakes and Isadore Traschen. Englewood Cliffs, N.J.: Prentice-Hall, 1959.

K 41
Literature: An Introduction, ed. Hollis Summers and Edgar Whan. New York: McGraw-Hill, 1960.

K 42*
Rendezvous   A Prose Reader, ed. John J. McShea and Jospeh W. Ratigan. New York: Scribners, 1960.

K 43
Stories of Modern America, ed. Herbert Gold and David L. Stevenson. Alter. ed. New York: St. Martin's, 1961.

K 44
Modern Short Stories   The Uses of Imagination, ed. Arthur Mizener. New York: Norton, 1962.

K 45*
Fifty Best American Short Stories: 1915–1965, ed. Martha Foley. Boston: Houghton Mifflin, 1965.

K 46
Galaxy, ed. Mark Schorer. New York: Harcourt, Brace & World, 1967.

K 47*
Reading Modern Fiction: 31 Stories with Critical Aids, ed. Winifred Lynskey. 4th ed. New York: Scribners, 1968. (Earlier editions not seen.)

K 48
Stories from the Quarto, ed. Leonard Stanley Brown. New York: Scribners, 1968.

K 49
American Literature, Vol. II, ed. Richard Poirier and William L. Vance. Boston: Little, Brown, 1970.

K 50*
Exploring Literature, ed. Lynn Altenbernd. New York: Macmillan, 1970.

K 51*
Collection Literature for the Seventies, ed. Gerald Messner and Nancy S. Messner. Lexington, Mass.: Heath, 1971, 1972.

K 52*
Literature in America, Vol. III, ed. Robert C. Albrecht. New York: Free Press, 1971.

K 53*
Literary Types and Themes, ed. Maurice B. McNamee, James E. Cronin, and Joseph A. Rogers. New York: Holt, Rinehart & Winston, 1971.

K 54*
The Age of Anxiety: Modern American Stories, ed. C. Jeriel Howard and Richard Francis Tracz. Boston: Allyn & Bacon, 1972.

K 55*
Coming Together Modern Stories by Black and White Americans, ed. Adam A. Casmier and Sally Souder. Encino & Belmont, Calif.: Dickenson, 1972.

K 56
Great Short Stories of the World. Pleasantville, N.Y.: The Reader's Digest Association, 1972.

K 57*
Rites, ed. John Cafferata. New York: McGraw-Hill, 1974, 1975.

K 58*
Major American Short Stories, ed. A. Walton Litz. New York: Oxford University Press, 1975.

K 59*
The Short Story: An Introductory Anthology, ed. Robert A. Rees and Barry Menikoff. 2nd ed. Boston: Little, Brown, 1975.

K 60*
Initiation: Stories and Short Novels on Three Themes, ed. David Thorburn. 2nd ed. New York: Harcourt Brace Jovanovich, 1976.

K 61*
The Modern Tradition   An Anthology of Short Stories, ed. Daniel F. Howard. 3rd ed. Boston: Little, Brown, 1976.

K 62*
An Introduction to Literature, ed. Sylvan Barnet, Morton Berman, and William Burto. 6th ed. Boston: Little, Brown, 1977.

K 63*
Elements of Literature, ed. Robert Scholes, Carl Klaus, and Michael Silverman. New York: Oxford University Press, 1978.

K 64*
Fiction's Journey   50 Stories, ed. Barbara McKenzie. New York: Harcourt Brace Jovanovich, 1978.

K 65*
The Norton Anthology of Short Fiction, ed. R. V. Cassill. New York: Norton, 1978.

K 66*
The Norton Anthology of Short Fiction, ed. R. V. Cassill. Shorter ed. New York: Norton, 1978.

K 67
The Scribner Quarto of Modern Literature, ed. A. Walton Litz. New York: Scribners, 1978.

"THE BABY PARTY" (STORY)

K 68
Editor's Choice, ed. Alfred Dashiell. New York: Putnam, 1934.

K 69*
A World of Great Stories, ed. Hiram Haydn and John Cournos. New York: Crown, 1947.

K 70*
Welcome to Life, ed. H. S. Burnett and Eleanor Gilchrist. New York: Fell, 1948.

K 71
American Short Stories, ed. Eugene Current-García and Walton R. Patrick. Rev. ed. Chicago: Scott, Foresman, 1952*, 1964, 1976*.

K 72*
Modern American Humor, ed. Bennett Cerf. Garden City, N.Y.: Doubleday, 1954.

K 73*
Literature for Interpretation, ed. Wallace A. Bacon and Robert S. Breen. New York: Holt, Rinehart & Winston, 1961.

K 74
The Story at Work: An Anthology, ed. Jessie C. Rehder. New York: Odyssey Press, 1963.

K 75*
Adventures in American Literature, ed. James Early et al. New York: Harcourt, Brace & World, 1968.

K 76*
An Introduction to Fiction, ed. X. J. Kennedy. Boston: Little, Brown, 1976.

"BASIL AND CLEOPATRA" (STORY)

K 77*
Prose and Criticism, ed. John Hamilton McCallum. New York: Harcourt, Brace & World, 1966.

"THE BEAUTIFUL AND DAMNED" (NOVEL)

K 78
The American Treasury 1455–1955, ed. Clifton Fadiman and Charles Van Doren. New York: Harper, 1955.

Excerpt. See A 8.6‡.

K 79
The Classic Woman, ed. James Sterling Moran. New York: Playboy Press, 1971.

Excerpts. See A 8.7‡.

"BENEDICTION" (STORY)

K 80*
The Smart Set Anthology, ed. B. Rascoe and G. Conklin. New York: Reynal & Hitch-cock, 1934.

K 81
Great Modern Catholic Short Stories, ed. Sister Mariella Gable. New York: Sheed & Ward, 1942.

K 82*
They Are People, ed. Sister Mariella Gable. New York: Sheed & Ward, 1943; London: Sheed & Ward, 1944.

K 83*
Bachelor's Companion, ed. B. Rascoe and G. Conklin. New York: Grayson, 1944.

K 84
Twelve Great Stories   A New Anthology (Avon Short Story Monthly), no. 31 (June 1946).

K 85
Golden Legends, ed. Samuel Cummings. New York: Pellegrini & Cudahy, 1948.

K 86*
Angles of Vision, ed. Edward Huberman and Robert Raymo. Boston: Houghton Mifflin, 1962.

"BERNICE BOBS HER HAIR" (STORY)

K 87*
Stories, ed. Frank G. Jennings and Charles J. Calitri. New York: Harcourt, Brace, 1957.

K 88*
The United States in Literature, ed. James E. Miller, Jr., Robert Hayden, and Robert O'Neal. Glenview, Ill.: Scott, Foresman, 1973.

K 89
The Saturday Evening Post, CCXLVIII (July/August 1976).

K 90
The American Short Story, ed. Calvin Skaggs. New York: Dell, 1977.

With screenplay by Joan Micklin Silver.

"THE BOWL" (STORY)

K 91
Stories for Men   The Fourth Round, ed. Charles Grayson. New York: Holt, 1953.

Earlier editions reprinted "A Short Trip Home." See B 36, K 341‡.

"THE BOY WHO KILLED HIS MOTHER" (POEM)

K 92
Neurotica, ed. Jay Irving Landesman and Gershon Legman. New York: Hacker, 1963.

See B 57.

K 93
Ellery Queen's Mystery Magazine, XLIV (November 1964).

"THE CAMEL'S BACK" (STORY)

K 94
O. Henry Memorial Award Prize Stories of 1920. Garden City, N.Y. & Toronto: Doubleday, Page, 1921.

See B 2.

K 95
Best American Stories, 1919–1924, Vol. I, ed. Blanche Colton Williams. Garden City, N.Y.: Doubleday, Page, 1926.

"THE CAMEO FRAME I" (POEM)

K 96
"Past Poetic," *University*, VIII (Spring 1961).

"THE CAMEO FRAME II" (POEM)

K 97
"Past Poetic," *University*, VIII (Spring 1961).

"THE CAPTURED SHADOW" (STORY)

K 98
The Scholastic, XXVII (12 October 1935).

K 99*
Short Stories for English Courses, ed. Rosa Mary Mikels and Helen T. Munn. Rev. ed. New York: Scribners, 1960.

K 100
Short Stories for English Courses, ed. R. M. R. Mikels, New York: Scribners, 1963.

"THE CRACK-UP" (ESSAY)

K 101
The American Treasury 1455–1955, ed. Clifton Fadiman and Charles Van Doren. New York: Harper, 1955.

Excerpts.

K 102
Major Writers of America, Vol. II, ed. Perry Miller. New York: Harcourt, Brace & World, 1962.

K 103
A New Directions Reader, ed. Hayden Carruth and J. Laughlin. New York: New Directions, 1964.

K 104
American Literary Masters, Vol. II, ed. Charles R. Anderson. New York: Holt, Rinehart & Winston, 1965.

K 105
Twentieth Century American Writing, ed. William T. Stafford. New York: Odyssey Press, 1965.

Excerpt.

K 106
Major Writers of America, ed. Perry Miller. Shorter ed. New York: Harcourt, Brace & World, 1966.

K 107
Essays Classic & Contemporary, ed. R. W. Lid. Philadelphia: Lippincott, 1967.

K 108
American Perspectives, ed. Harold P. Simonson. New York: McGraw-Hill, 1968.

K 109
American Literature   The Makers and the Making, Vol. II, ed. Cleanth Brooks, R. W. B. Lewis, and Robert Penn Warren. New York: St. Martin's, 1973.

"CRAZY SUNDAY" (STORY)

K 110
The Best Short Stories 1933, ed. Edward J. O'Brien. Boston: Houghton Mifflin, 1933.
See B 17.

K 111
The American Mercury Reader, ed. Lawrence E. Spivak and Charles Angoff. Philadelphia: Blakiston, 1944; Garden City, N.Y.: Blue Ribbon Books, 1946.

K 112*
Avon Short Story Monthly, no. 42 (July 1948).

K 113*
Great Stories about Show Business, ed. Jerry D. Lewis. New York: Coward-McCann, 1957.

K 114
Concerning a Woman of Sin and Other Stories of Hollywood, ed. Daniel Talbot. Greenwich, Conn.: Fawcett, 1960.

K 115*
Story: An Introduction to Prose Fiction, ed. Arthur Foff and Daniel Knapp. Belmont, Calif.: Wadsworth, 1964.

K 116
Twentieth Century American Writing, ed. William T. Stafford. New York: Odyssey Press, 1965.

K 117*
The Unity of Prose   From Description to Allegory, ed. Stanley Stewart. New York: Harper & Row, 1968.

"THE CURIOUS CASE OF BENJAMIN BUTTON" (STORY)

K 118
Pause to Wonder, ed. Marjorie Fischer and Rolfe Humphries. New York: Messner, 1944.

K 119*
Avon Ghost Reader, no. A-90 (September 1946).

K 120
Travelers in Time: Strange Tales of Man's Journeyings into the Past and Future, ed.
Philip Van Doren Stern. New York: Doubleday, 1947.

K 121*
The Treasury of Science Fiction Classics, ed. Harold W. Kuebler. Garden City, N.Y.:
Hanover House, 1954.

K 122*
The Design of Fiction, ed Mark Harris, Josephine Harris, and Hester Harris. New York:
Crowell, 1976.

"DALYRIMPLE GOES WRONG" (STORY)

K 123*
Short Stories: A Critical Anthology, ed. Ensaf Thune and Ruth Prigozy. New York:
Macmillan, 1973.

"THE DANCE" (STORY)

K 124
Samples   A Collection of Short Stories. New York: Boni & Liveright, 1927.

See B 8.

K 125*
The Fabric of Fiction, ed. Douglas Bement and R. M. Taylor. New York: Harcourt,
Brace, 1943, 1946.

Excerpt.

K 126
Samples   14 Great Stories by 14 Great Authors (Avon Modern Short Story Monthly),
no. 7 (1943).

K 127
Ellery Queen's Mystery Magazine, XXI (March 1953).

K 128*
Coming Aphrodite. New York: Avon, 1955.

K 129
Ellery Queen's 1963 Anthology, ed. Ellery Queen. New York: Davis, 1962.

K 130
The Saint Mystery Magazine, IX, London ed. (May 1963); XIX, New York ed. (July
1963).

K 131*
The Lucifer Society   Macabre Tales by Great Modern Writers, ed. Peter Haining. New
York: Taplinger, 1972; London: Allen, 1972.

"DEARLY BELOVED" (STORY)

K 132
New York Times (20 August 1969).

K 133
Louisville Courier-Journal (21 August 1969).

K 134
Paris International Herald-Tribune (21 August 1969).

K 135
Akron Beacon Journal (14 September 1969).

K 136
San Francisco Examiner (21 September 1969).

K 137
London Daily Telegraph Magazine (28 November 1969).

K 138
NCR World, II (November–December 1969).

"THE DEBUTANTE" (STORY)

K 139
Nassau Lit. 1842–1942, C (1942).

K 140
The Smart Set, ed. Carl R. Dolmetsch. New York: Dial, 1966.

See B 62.

"DESIGN IN PLASTER" (STORY)

K 141
The Best Short Stories 1940, ed. Edward J. O'Brien. Boston: Houghton Mifflin, 1940.

See B 24.

"THE DIAMOND AS BIG AS THE RITZ" (STORY)

K 142
Modern American Prose, ed. Carl Van Doren. New York: Harcourt, Brace, 1934; New York: Literary Guild of America, 1934.

K 143*
The Moonlight Traveler: Great Tales of Fantasy and Imagination, ed. Philip Van Doren Stern. Garden City, N.Y.: Doubleday, Doran, 1943.

K 144
11 Great Modern Stories. New York: Avon, 1947.

K 145*
Great Tales of Fantasy and Imagination, ed. Philip Van Doren Stern. New York: Pocket Books, 1954.

K 146*
A Quarto of Modern Literature, ed. Leonard Brown and Porter G. Perrin. 4th ed. New York: Scribners, 1957.

K 147*
The Short Story: Fiction in Transition, ed. John Chesley Taylor. New York: Scribners, 1969.

K 148*
200 Years of Great American Short Stories, ed. Martha Foley. Boston: Houghton Mifflin, 1975.

"EARLY SUCCESS" (ESSAY)

K 149
Modern Prose Form and Style, ed. William Van O'Connor. New York: Crowell, 1959.

K 150
Metronome, LXXVII (September 1960).

K 151
The Modern Age Literature, ed. Leonard Lief and James F. Light. New York: Holt, Rinehart & Winston, 1969.

"ECHOES OF THE JAZZ AGE" (ESSAY)

K 152
These Were Our Years, ed. Frank Brookhouser. Garden City, N.Y.: Doubleday, 1959.

K 153
Major Writers of America, Vol. II, ed. Perry Miller. New York: Harcourt, Brace & World, 1962.

K 154
Off Campus, I (December 1962).

K 155
20th Century American Authors, ed. K. Ohashi and T. Koyama. Tokyo: Kinseido, 1964.

K 155a
Fitzgerald and the Jazz Age, ed. Malcolm and Robert Cowley. New York: Scribners, 1966.

K 156
Vogue, CLXII (December 1973).

K 157
American Literature, Vol. II, ed. Richard Poirier and William L. Vance. Boston: Little,
Brown, 1970.

K 158
The Culture of the Twenties, ed. Loren Baritz. Indianapolis & New York: Bobbs-Merrill,
1970.

"FAMILY IN THE WIND" (STORY)

K 159
O. Henry Memorial Award Prize Stories of 1933, ed. Harry Hansen. Garden City, N.Y.:
Doubleday, Doran, 1933.

See B 18.

K 160
A Treasury of Doctor Stories by the World's Great Authors, ed. Noah D. Fabricant and
Heinz Werner. New York: Fell, 1946.

"THE FIEND" (STORY)

K 161*
Way Out   A Thematic Reader, ed. Lois A. Michel. New York: Holt, Rinehart & Winston,
1968.

"FINANCING FINNEGAN" (STORY)

K 162*
The Fireside Treasury of Modern Humor, ed. Scott Meredith. New York: Simon &
Schuster, 1963.

"FITZGERALD BACK FROM RIVIERA . . ." (INTERVIEW)

K 163
The Left Bank Revisited, ed. Hugh Ford. University Park & London: Pennsylvania State
University Press, 1972.

See B 90‡.

"FLIGHT AND PURSUIT" (STORY)

K 164
Wives and Lovers, ed. Alex Austin. New York: Lion Library, 1956.

See B 83‡.

"THE FOUR FISTS" (STORY)

K 165*
For Men Only; A Collection of Short Stories, ed. James M. Cain. Cleveland: World, 1944.

K 166*
As I Pass, O Manhattan An Anthology of Life in New York, ed. Esther Morgan McCullough. North Bennington, Vt.: Taylor, 1956.

"THE FRESHEST BOY" (STORY)

K 167
The Story; A Critical Anthology, ed. Mark Schorer. New York: Prentice-Hall, 1950.

K 168*
College English: The First Year, ed. J. Hooper Wise et al. New York: Harcourt, Brace, 1952, 1956, 1960.

K 169*
The Story Survey, ed. Harold William Blodgett. Rev. ed. New York & Philadelphia: Lippincott, 1953.

K 170*
The Informal Reader A College Anthology, ed. T. C. Eaves and Ben D. Kimpel. New York: Appleton-Century-Crofts, 1955.

K 171
Selection A Reader for College Writing, ed. Walter Havighurst et al. New York: Dryden Press, 1955.

K 172*
Reading for Pleasure, ed. Bennett Cerf. New York: Harper, 1957.

K 173*
An Introduction to Literature: Reading the Short Story, ed. Herbert Barrows. Boston: Houghton Mifflin, 1959.

K 174*
Story and Structure, ed. Laurence Perrine. New York: Harcourt, Brace, 1959.

K 175*
Modern Short Stories: The Fiction of Experience, ed. M. X. Lesser and John N. Morris. New York: McGraw-Hill, 1962.

K 176*
The Best of Both Worlds, ed. Georgess McHargue, Garden City, N.Y.: Doubleday, 1968.

K 177*
A Variety of Short Stories, ed. John C. Schweitzer. New York: Scribners, 1968.

K 178*
Literature 1, ed. Emil Roy and Sandra Roy. New York: Macmillan, 1976.

K 179*
To Be Identity and Literature, ed. Edmund J. Farrell et al. Glenview, Ill.: Scott, Foresman, 1976.

K 180*
Papertexts, Advanced ser. New York: Simon & Schuster, n.d.

INTRODUCTION TO *THE GREAT GATSBY*

K 181
A Little Treasury of American Prose, ed. George Mayberry. New York: Scribners, 1949.

K 181a
Fitzgerald's The Great Gatsby, ed. Henry Dan Piper. New York: Scribners, 1970.

THE GREAT GATSBY (NOVEL)

K 182
The Great American Parade. Garden City, N.Y.: Doubleday, Doran, 1935.

Excerpt. See A 11.22.

K 183
North, East, South, West, ed. Charles Lee. New York: Soskin, 1945.

Excerpt. See A 11.23.

K 184
I Wish I'd Written That, ed. Eugene J. Woods. New York & London: Whittlesey House, 1946.

Excerpt. See A 11.24.

K 185
Taken at the Flood, ed. Ann Watkins. New York: Harper, 1946.

Excerpt. See A 11.31‡

K 186
Better Reading, II: Literature, ed. Walter Blair and John Gerber. Chicago: Scott, Foresman, 1948.

Excerpt. See A 11.32‡.

K 187
These Would I Choose, ed. Alec Waugh. London: Low, 1948.

Excerpts. See A 11.33‡.

K 188
Center, Stella S. *The Art of Book Reading.* New York: Scribners, 1952.

Excerpt. See A 11.34‡.

K 189
The American Treasury 1455–1955, ed. Clifton Fadiman and Charles Van Doren. New York: Harper, 1955.

Excerpt. See A 11.35‡.

K 190
An Anthology of American Humor, ed. Brom Weber. New York: Crowell, 1962.

Excerpt. see A 11.36‡.

K 191
Advanced Spanish Composition, ed. Cyril A. Janes and Alec Payne. London: Oxford University Press, 1971.

Excerpt. See A 11.37‡.

K 192
In the Presence of This Continent, ed. Robert Baylor and James Moore. New York: Holt, Rinehart & Winston, 1971.

Epigraph. See A 11.38‡.

K 192a
The Saturday Evening Post Automobile Book. Indianapolis: Curtis, 1977.

Excerpt. See A 11.39‡.

"GRETCHEN'S FORTY WINKS" (STORY)

K 193
Aces   A Collection of Short Stories. New York & London: Putnam, 1924.

See B 4.

"HANDLE WITH CARE" (ESSAY)

K 194
The American Treasury 1455–1955, ed. Clifton Fadiman and Charles Van Doren. New York: Harper, 1955.

Excerpt.

"HAS THE FLAPPER CHANGED?" (ARTICLE)

K 195
Spellbound in Darkness, by George C. Pratt. Rochester, N.Y.: University of Rochester, 1966; Greenwich, Conn.: New York Graphic Society, 1973.

See B 85‡.

"HOT AND COLD BLOOD" (STORY)

K 196*
Today's Woman, XIV (September 1946).

"HOW TO LIVE ON $36,000 A YEAR" (ESSAY)

K 197
75 Prose Pieces, ed. Robert C. Rathburn and Martin Steinmann, Jr. 2nd ed. New York: Scribners, 1961*, 1967.

"HOW TO WASTE MATERIAL: A NOTE ON MY GENERATION" (ESSAY-REVIEW)

K 198
The Griffin, VII (Summer 1958).

"THE ICE PALACE" (STORY)

K 199
Trumps: A Collection of Short Stories. New York & London: Putnam 1926.

K 200*
The Fabric of Fiction, ed. Douglas Bement and R. M. Taylor. New York: Harcourt Brace, 1943, 1946.

Excerpt.

K 201*
Modern Short Stories, ed. Jim Hunter. London: Faber & Faber, 1964, 1966.

K 202
Major Writers of America, ed. Perry Miller. Shorter ed. New York: Harcourt, Brace & World, 1966.

K 203*
Ten Modern American Short Stories, ed. David Galloway and John Whitley. London: Methuen, 1968.

K 204*
Not Quite Twenty   Stories, Poems, and a Play, ed. Ruth F. Eisenberg. New York: Holt, Rinehart & Winston, 1971.

K 205*
Comparisons   A Short Story Anthology, ed. Nicolaus Mills. New York: McGraw-Hill, 1972.

K 206*
Social Psychology Through Literature, ed. Ronald Fernandez. New York: Wiley, 1972.

K 207*
Four Modes: A Rhetoric of Modern Fiction, ed. James M. Mellard. New York: Macmillan, 1973.

"IMAGINATION—AND A FEW MOTHERS" (ESSAY)

K 208
The Ladies' Home Journal Treasury, ed. John Mason Brown et al. New York: Simon & Schuster, 1956.

See B 43.

"AN INTERVIEW WITH F. SCOTT FITZGERALD" (SELF-INTERVIEW)

K 209
Books and Bookmen, IX (June 1964).

"THE INTIMATE STRANGERS" (STORY)

K 210
McCall's, CIII, 100th Aniversary Issue (April 1976).

"THE INVASION OF THE SANCTUARY" (ESSAY)

K 211
Ideas for Writing, by Kenneth L. Knickerbocker. New York: Holt, 1951, 1953.

See B 33.

"THE JELLY-BEAN" (STORY)

K 212*
Contemporary Types of the Short Story, ed. G. H. Gerould and Charles Bayly, Jr. New York: Harper, 1927.

K 213
Contemporary Trends   American Literature Since 1914, ed. John Herbert Nelson. New York: Macmillan, 1933.

K 214
Reading the Short Story, ed. Harry Shaw and Douglas Bement. New York & London: Harper, 1941, 1954.

K 215*
The Fabric of Fiction, ed. Douglas Bement and R. M. Taylor. New York: Harcourt, Brace, 1943, 1946.

K 216*
Craft of the Short Story, ed. Richard Summers. New York: Rinehart, 1948.

K 217
College Reading   A Collection of Prose, Plays, and Poetry, ed. George Sanderlin. Boston: Heath, 1953*, 1958.

K 218*
Fifty Modern Stories, ed. Thomas M. H. Blair et al. Evanston, Ill.: Row, Peterson, 1960; New York: Harper & Row, 1960.

K 219*
The Golden Shore, ed. William Peden. New York: Platt & Munk, 1967.

K 220*
Contemporary American Thought   A College Reader, ed. E. W. Johnson. New York: Free Press, 1968.

K 221*
Anthology: An Introduction to Literature, ed. Lynn Altenbernd. New York: Macmillan, 1977.

"JEMINA" (STORY)

K 222
Nassau Lit. 1842–1942, C (1942).

"THE LAST KISS" (STORY)

K 223
Great Tales of the Far West, ed. Alex Austin. New York: Lion Library, 1956.

See B 41.

K 224
A Cavalcade of Collier's, ed. Kenneth McArdle. New York: Barnes, 1959.

"THE LAST OF THE BELLES" (STORY)

K 225
Reading Modern Fiction, ed. Winifred Lynskey. New York: Scribners, 1952, 1957.

K 226*
Mainstream   Modern Short Stories, Vol. II, ed. Frank Whitehead. London: Chatto & Windus, 1967.

K 227*
Ten of the Best—Selected Short Stories, ed. John Brennan. London: Faber & Faber, 1969.

K 228
Images of Women in Literature, ed. Mary Anne Ferguson. Boston: Houghton Mifflin, 1973.

"THE LAST TYCOON" (UNFINISHED NOVEL)

K 229
In the Presence of This Continent, ed. Robert Baylor and James Moore. New York: Holt, Rinehart & Winston, 1971.

Excerpt. See A 18.7‡.

"THE LONG WAY OUT" (STORY)

K 230*
The Realm of Fiction, ed. James B. Hall. New York: McGraw-Hill, 1965.

K 231*
Literature for Writing—An Anthology of Major British and American Authors, ed. Martin Steinmann and Gerald Willen. Belmont, Calif.: Wadsworth, 1967.

K 232*
American Short Fiction: Readings and Criticism, ed. James K. Bowen and Richard Van Der Beets. Indianapolis, Ind.: Bobbs-Merrill, 1970.

"LOOKING BACK EIGHT YEARS" (ESSAY)

K 233
Liberty/Then & Now, I (Summer 1974).

"THE LOST DECADE" (STORY)

K 234*
31 Stories, ed. Michael R. Booth and Clinton S. Burhans, Jr., Englewood Cliffs, N.J.: Prentice-Hall, 1960.

K 235
20th Century American Authors, ed. K. Ohashi and T. Koyama. Tokyo: Kinseido, 1964.

K 236*
The Bitter Years—The Thirties in Literature, ed. Max Bogart. New York: Scribners, 1969.

K 237*
The Variety of Fiction: A Critical Anthology, ed. Edward A. Bloom and Lillian D. Bloom. New York: Odyssey Press, 1969.

"MAGNETISM" (STORY)

K 238
Read with Me, ed. Thomas B. Costain. New York: Literary Guild of America, 1965.

"MARCHING STREETS" (POEM)

K 239
A Book of Princeton Verse, II, ed. Henry Van Dyke et al. Princeton: Princeton University Press; London: Humphrey Milford & Oxford University Press, 1919.

See B 1.

K 240
Nassau Lit. 1842–1942, C (1942).

"MAY DAY" (STORY)

K 241
This Generation, ed. G. K. Anderson and E. L. Walton. Chicago: Scott, Foresman, 1939.

K 242
American Literary Masters, Vol. II, ed. Charles R. Anderson. New York: Holt, Rinehart & Winston, 1965.

K 243*
New York New York—The City as Seen by Masters of Art and Literature, ed. John Gordon and L. Rust Hills. New York: Shorecrest, 1965.

K 244
Short Story: A Thematic Anthology, ed. Dorothy Parker and Frederick B. Shroyer. New York: Scribners, 1965.

K 245*
Seven Novellas, ed. Marsden V. Dillenbeck and John C. Schweitzer. New York: Scribners, 1966.

"A MILLIONAIRE'S GIRL" (STORY)

K 246
Great Tales of City Dwellers, ed. Alex Austin. New York: Lion Library, 1955; Pyramid, 1963. Mostly by Zelda Fitzgerald.

See B 39.

"MY FIRST LOVE" (POEM)

K 247
A Book of Princeton Verse II, ed. Henry Van Dyke et al. Princeton: Princeton University Press; London: Humphrey Milford & Oxford University Press, 1919.

See B 1.

"MY GENERATION" (ESSAY)

K 248
Profile of F. Scott Fitzgerald, ed. Matthew J. Bruccoli. Columbus, Ohio: Merrill, 1971.

See B 76.

K 249
Esquire, LXXX (October 1973).

K 250
Esquire   The Best of 40 Years. New York: McKay, 1973.

"MY LOST CITY" (ESSAY)

K 251
A Collection of Travel in America by Various Hands, ed. George Bradshaw. New York: Farrar, Straus, 1948.

K 252*
Empire City, ed. Alexander Klein. New York: Rinehart, 1955.

K 253
The Best from Cosmopolitan, ed. Richard Gehman. New York: Avon, 1961.

K 254
Themes from Experience   A Manual of Literature for Writers, ed. William E. Buckler. New York: Norton, 1962.

K 255
The Personal Voice, ed. A. J. Guerard. New York & Philadelphia: Lippincott, 1964.

K 256
Eastern Review, II (April 1977).

"MY OLD NEW ENGLAND HOMESTEAD ON THE ERIE" (ARTICLE)

K 257
You—At Twenty. New York: College Humor, 1927.

See B 9.

"THE MYSTERY OF THE RAYMOND MORTGAGE" (STORY)

K 258
Ellery Queen's 15th Mystery Annual, ed. Ellery Queen. New York: Random House, 1960; London: Gollancz, 1961.

See B 52.

K 259
Ellery Queen's Mystery Magazine, XXXV (March 1960).

K 260*
Down a Dark Street, ed. C. E. J. Smith. London: Arnold, 1973.

"A NEW LEAF" (STORY)

K 261
The Best American Love Stories of the Year, ed. Margaret Widdemer. New York: Day, 1932.

See B 16.

"THE NIGHT BEFORE CHANCELLORSVILLE" (STORY)

K 262
The Bedside Esquire, ed. Arnold Gingrich. New York: McBride, 1940; New York: Tudor, 1940; London & Toronto: Heinemann, 1941; New York: Grosset & Dunlap, 1946; London: Barker, 1946; Sydney & London: Angus & Robertson, 1952.

K 263
Best of the Bedside Esquire, ed. Arnold Gingrich. New York: Bantam, 1954.

K 264
The Night Before Chancellorsville and Other Civil War Stories, ed. Shelby Foote. New York: New American Library, 1957.

MATERIAL FROM THE NOTE-BOOKS (*THE CRACK-UP*)

K 265
"Fitzgerald's Recipes for Turkey from *The Crack-Up,*" *Gourmet* (November 1959).

K 266
American Literature   The Makers and the Making, Vol. II, ed. Cleanth Brooks, R. W. B. Lewis, and Robert Penn Warren. New York: St. Martin's, 1973.

Excerpts.

"NOT IN THE GUIDEBOOK" (STORY)

K 267*
Golden Book, IX (February 1929).

"OBIT ON PARNASSUS" (POEM)

K 268
Innocent Merriment, ed. Franklin P. Adams. New York & London: McGraw-Hill, 1942; New York: Armed Services Editions, 1945(?).

See B 25.

K 269
What Cheer, ed. David McCord. New York: Coward-McCann, 1945; New York: Modern Library, 1955.

K 270*
Pocket Book of Humorous Verse, ed. David McCord. New York: Pocket Books, 1946.

"THE OFFSHORE PIRATE" (STORY)

K 271
Love Stories, ed. Martin Levin. New York: Quadrangle, 1975.

"ON A PLAY TWICE SEEN" (POEM)

K 272
"Past Poetic," *University,* VIII (Spring 1961).

"ONE INTERNE" (STORY)

K 273*
Doctor's Choice; Sixteen Stories about Doctors and Medicine Selected by Famous Physicians, ed. Albert P. Blaustein and Phyllis Blaustein. New York: Funk, 1957; London: Allen, 1958.

"ONE OF MY OLDEST FRIENDS" (STORY)

K 274
The World's Best Short Stories of 1926. New York: Doran, 1926.

See B 6.

K 275*
Golden Book, IX (February 1929).

K 276*
A Diamond of Years, ed. Helen Otis Lamont. Garden City, N.Y.: Doubleday, 1961.

"THE PASSIONATE ESKIMO" (STORY)

K 277*
Famous Short Stories, Vol. I, ed. Kurt Singer. Minneapolis, Minn.: Denison, 1968.

K 278
Showpiece, I (July, August, September 1972).

"PASTING IT TOGETHER" (ESSAY)

K 279
The American Treasury 1455–1955, ed. Clifton Fadiman and Charles Van Doren. New York: Harper, 1955.

Excerpt.

K 280
Esquire, LXXX (October 1973).

K 281
Esquire   The Best of 40 Years. New York: McKay, 1973.

"PAT HOBBY'S CHRISTMAS WISH" (STORY)

K 282
The Equire Treasury, ed. Arnold Gingrich. New York: Simon & Schuster, 1953; London: Heinemann, 1954.

See B 38.

"A PATRIOTIC SHORT" (STORY)

K 283
Best Movie Stories, ed. Guy Slater. London: Faber & Faber, 1969.

K 284
Subject and Structure   An Anthology for Writers, ed. John M. Wasson. 5th ed. Boston: Little, Brown, 1975. (Earlier editions not seen.)

"A PENNY SPENT" (STORY)

K 285*
Modern Woman, CXI (September 1926).

"THE PIERIAN SPRINGS AND THE LAST STRAW" (STORY)

K 286
Kuehl, John. "A Note on the Begetting of *Gatsby,*" *University,* XXI (Summer 1964).

K 287
"An Early Scott Fitzgerald Rediscovered," *Washington Post* (27 December 1964).

"THE POPE AT CONFESSION" (POEM)

K 288
A Book of Princeton Verse II, ed. Henry Van Dyke et al. Princeton: Princeton University Press; London: Humphrey Milford & Oxford University Press, 1919.

See B 1.

"THE POPULAR GIRL" (STORY)

K 288a
A Collection of Travel in America by Various Hands, ed. George Bradshaw. New York: Farrar, Straus, 1948.

Excerpt.

"PRINCETON" (ESSAY)

K 289
Ten Years of Princeton '17, ed. Wells Drorbaugh, James S. Warren, and Harvey H. Smith. Princeton: Class of 1917, 1929.

See B 10.

K 290
1917's 40th. Princeton: Class of 1917, 1957.

K 291*
The College Years, ed. A. C. Spectorsky. New York: Hawthorn, 1958.

K 292
1917's 50th. Princeton: Class of 1917, 1967.

Excerpt.

"THE PUSHER-IN-THE-FACE" (STORY)

K 293
Cream of the Jug, ed. Grant Overton. New York & London: Harper, 1927.

See B 7.

K 294*
Golden Book, VII (February 1928).

K 295
Recent Short Stories, ed. Margaret Pendleton and David Schermerhorn Wilkins. New York: Appleton, 1928.

"RAIN BEFORE DAWN" (POEM)

K 296
"Past Poetic," *University,* VIII (Spring 1961).

"READE, SUBSTITUTE RIGHT HALF" (STORY)

K 297
The Princeton University Library Chronicle, XVII (Autumn 1955).

"THE RICH BOY" (STORY)

K 298
Present-Day American Stories. New York: Scribners, 1929.

K 299
The Bedside Book of Famous American Stories, ed. Angus Burrell and Bennett A. Cerf. New York: Random House, 1936.

K 300*
Tellers of Tales, ed. W. Somerset Maugham. New York: Doubleday, Doran, 1939.

K 301
The Literature of the United States, Vol. II, ed. Walter Blair et al. Chicago: Scott, Foresman, 1946*, 1947*, 1949*, 1957, 1961*, 1966. (The 1957 printing is a revised single-volume edition.)

K 302*
The Golden Argosy, ed. Charles Grayson and Van H. Cartmell. New York: Dial, 1947, 1955; Garden City, N.Y.: Garden City Publishing, 1949; New York: Bantam, 1956.

K 303
The Greatest Stories of All Time, ed. W. Somerset Maugham. Garden City, N.Y.: Garden City Publishing, 1947.

K 304
The Pocket Treasury, ed. Louis Untermeyer et al. New York: Pocket Books, 1947.

K 305*
A College Book of American Literature; Briefer Course, ed. Milton Ellis et al. 2nd ed. New York: American Book Co., 1949.

K 306
The Perma Week-End Companion, ed. Edwin Valentine Mitchell. New York: Perma-books, 1950.

K 307
A Quarto of Modern Literature, ed. Leonard Brown and Porter G. Perrin. 3rd ed. New York: Scribners, 1950.

Earlier editions reprinted "Babylon Revisited." See K 15‡.

K 308
Modern American Literature, ed. Bernard I. Duffey. New York: Rinehart, 1951*; Holt, Rinehart & Winston, 1962.

K 309
The American Twenties   A Literary Panorama, ed. John K. Hutchens. New York & Philadelphia: Lippincott, 1952.

K 310
An Approach to Literature, ed. Cleanth Brooks, John Thibaut Purser, and Robert Penn Warren. New York: Appleton-Century-Crofts, 1952*, 1964.

K 311*
Major American Writers, ed. Howard Mumford Jones, Ernest Leisy, and Richard M. Ludwig. 3rd ed. New York: Harcourt, Brace, 1952.

K 312
An Anthology of Famous American Stories, ed. Angus Burrell and Bennett A. Cerf. New York: Modern Library, 1953.

K 313*
Literature for Our Time, ed. Harlow O. Waite and Benjamin P. Atkinson. Rev. ed. New York: Holt, 1953.

K 314
The American Treasury 1455–1955, ed. Clifton Fadiman and Charles Van Doren. New York: Harper, 1955.

Excerpt.

K 315*
Stories from Literature for Our Time, ed. Harlow O. Waite and Benjamin P. Atkinson. Rev. ed. New York: Holt, 1956.

K 316
The American Literary Record, ed. Willard Thorp et al. New York & Philadelphia: Lippincott, 1961.

K 317
Major Writers of America, Vol. II, ed. Perry Miller. New York: Harcourt, Brace & World, 1962.

K 318
Studies in Fiction, ed. Blaze O. Bonazza and Emil Roy. New York: Harper & Row, 1965.

K 319
An Anthology of American Literature, ed. Thomas M. Davis and Willoughby Johnson. Indianapolis & New York: Bobbs-Merrill, 1966.

K 320*
Modern American Classics: An Anthology of Short Fiction, ed. David R. Weimer. New York: Random House, 1969.

K 321*
The Penguin Book of American Short Stories, ed. James Cochrane. Harmondsworth: Penguin, 1969.

K 322
The Short Story: An Introductory Anthology, ed. Robert A. Rees and Barry Menikoff. Boston: Little, Brown, 1969.

K 323*
American Poetry and Prose, ed. Norman Foerster et al. 5th ed. Boston: Houghton Mifflin, 1970.

K 324
The Genius of American Fiction, ed. William Wasserstrom. Boston: Allyn & Bacon, 1970.

K 325*
Introduction to American Poetry and Prose, ed. Norman Foerster et al. 5th and 6th eds. Boston: Houghton Mifflin, 1970, 1971.

K 326*
Types of Short Fiction, ed. Roy R. Male. 2nd ed. Belmont, Calif.: Wadsworth, 1970.

K 327
American Literature   The Makers and the Making, Vol. II, ed. Cleanth Brooks, R. W. B. Lewis, and Robert Penn Warren. New York: St. Martin's, 1973.

K 328*
Anthology of American Literature, Vol. II, ed. George McMichael et al. New York: Macmillan, 1974.

K 329*
Concise Anthology of American Literature, ed. George McMichael et al. New York: Macmillan, 1974.

"RING" (ESSAY)

K 330
The New Republic Anthology, ed. Groff Conklin. New York: Dodge, 1936.

See B 21.

K 331
New Republic, CXXXI, 40th Anniversary Issue (22 November 1954).

K 332
Major Writers of America, Vol. II, ed. Perry Miller. New York: Harcourt, Brace & World, 1962.

K 333
The Faces of 5 Decades, ed. Robert B. Luce. New York: Simon & Schuster, 1964.

K 334
The Critic as Artist, ed. Gilbert A. Harrison. New York: Liveright, 1972.

"THE ROUGH CROSSING" (STORY)

K 335
Young Man Axelbrod & Other Stories, ed. Hiroshige Yoshida and Akio Maruta. Tokyo: Eihōsha, n.d.

"THE SCANDAL DETECTIVES" (STORY)

K 336*
The Tehran [Iran] *Journal* (3 September 1957).

Story was continued in subsequent issues.

"SEND ME IN, COACH" (STORY)

K 337
Esquire's 2nd Sports Reader, ed. Arnold Gingrich. New York: Barnes, 1946.
See B 27.

" 'THE SENSIBLE THING' " (STORY)

K 338
Understanding Fiction, ed. Cleanth Brooks and Robert Penn Warren. New York: Crofts,
1943*; New York: Appleton-Century-Crofts, 1959.

K 339
The Short Story   Ideas and Backgrounds, ed. Louis E. Glorfeld, Robert N. Broadus,
and Tom E. Kakonis. Columbus, Ohio: Merrill, 1967.

"A SHORT AUTOBIOGRAPHY" (ESSAY)

K 340
The New Yorker Scrapbook. Garden City, N.Y.: Doubleday, Doran, 1931.
See B 14.

"A SHORT TRIP HOME" (STORY)

K 341
Stories for Men, ed. Charles Grayson. Boston: Little, Brown, 1936; Garden City, N.Y.:
Garden City Publishing, 1944; New York: Armed Services Editions, 1945(?).

"The Bowl" was substituted for this story in the 1953 edition. See K 91‡.

K 342*
Modern Short Stories, ed. Emma L. Reppert and Clarence Stratton. New York & London: McGraw-Hill, 1939.

K 343
World's Great Mystery Stories   American and English Masterpieces, ed. Will Cuppy.
Cleveland & New York: World, 1943.

K 344
Rex Stout's Mystery Monthly, no. 7 (December 1946).

K 345
A Little Treasury of American Prose, ed. George Mayberry. New York: Scribners, 1949.

K 346
Stories for here and now, ed. Joseph Greene and Elizabeth Abell. New York: Bantam, 1951.

K 347*
Alfred Hitchcock Presents Stories My Mother Never Told Me, ed. Alfred Hitchcock. New York: Random House, 1963.

" 'SHOW MR. AND MRS. F. TO NUMBER——' " (ESSAY)

K 348
Abroad Travel Stories, Alan Ross. London: Faber & Faber, 1957.

"THE SWIMMERS" (STORY)

K 349
The American Treasury 1455–1955, ed. Clifton Fadiman and Charles Van Doren. New York: Harper, 1955.

Excerpt.

K 349a
Gunther, John. *Inside U.S.A.* New York: Harper, 1947.

TENDER IS THE NIGHT (NOVEL)

K 350
Reading Writing and Rewriting, ed. W. T. Moynihan et al. Philadelphia & New York: Lippincott, 1964.

Excerpt. See A 14.9‡.

K 350a
Fitzgerald and the Jazz Age, ed. Malcolm and Robert Cowley. New York: Scribners, 1966.

Excerpt. See A 14.10.

K 351
Cole, ed. Robert Kimball and Brendan Gill. New York, Chicago, & San Francisco: Holt, Rinehart & Winston, 1971.

Excerpt. See A 14.10‡.

K 352
The Novel, ed. Richard Freedman. New York: Newsweek Books, 1975.

Excerpt. See A 14.11‡.

PREFACE TO *THIS SIDE OF PARADISE* (NOVEL)

K 353
Antaeus, XXIV (Winter 1976).

THIS SIDE OF PARADISE (NOVEL)

K 354
Modern Women in Love, ed. Christina Stead and William Blake. New York: Dryden Press, 1945.

Excerpt. See A 5.11‡.

K 355
Swank (January 1946).

Excerpt.

K 356
Approaches to Prose, ed. Caroline Shrodes and Justine Van Gundy. New York: Macmillan, 1959.

Excerpt. See A 5.12‡.

K 357
Readings in American Literature, ed. Sabina Jędraszko. Warsaw: Pánstwowo Wydawnictwo Naukowe, 1961.

Excerpt. See A 5.10.

K 357a
Fitzgerald and the Jazz Age, ed. Malcolm and Robert Cowley. New York: Scribners, 1966.

Excerpt. See A 5.13.

"THOUSAND-AND-FIRST SHIP" (POEM)

K 358
The Golden Journey Poems for Young People, ed. Louise Bogan and William Jay Smith. Chicago: Reilly & Lee, 1965.

Excerpt.

"THREE ACTS OF MUSIC" (STORY)

K 359
The Armchair Esquire, ed. Arnold Gingrich and L. Rust Hills. New York: Putnam, 1958; London, Melbourne, & Toronto: Heinemann, 1959; New York: Popular Library, 1960.

See B 47.

"THREE HOURS BETWEEN PLANES" (STORY)

K 360*
Esquire, XXXIII (February 1950).

K 361
[Long Island, N.Y.] *Newsday* (24 March 1951).

"TWO FOR A CENT" (STORY)

K 362
The Best Short Stories of 1922, ed. Edward J. O'Brien. Boston: Small, Maynard, 1923; Toronto: Goodchild, 1923.

See B 3.

K 363
Short Stories for Class Reading, ed. Ralph P. Boas and Barbara M. Hahn. New York: Holt, 1925.

K 364*
Contemporary Types of the Short Story, ed. G. H. Gerould and Charles Bayly, Jr. New York: Harper, 1927.

K 365
Golden Book, XXI (February 1935).

K 366
The Fabric of Fiction, ed. Douglas Bement and R. M. Taylor. New York: Harcourt, Brace, 1943, 1946.

Excerpt.

"TWO OLD-TIMERS"

K 367
Modern Reading Number Eight, ed. Reginald Moore. London: Wells Gardner, Darton, 1944.

See B 26.

"UNDER FIRE" (REVIEW)

K 367a
Boyd, Thomas. *Through the Wheat*. Carbondale & Edwardsville: Southern Illinois University Press, 1978.

"VOYELLES" (POEM TRANSLATION)

K 368
The Penguin Book of Modern Verse Translation, ed. George Steiner. Harmondsworth: Penguin, 1966; Baltimore: Penguin, 1966.

See B 63.

K 369
"Documentary: 'Voyelles,' by Arthur Rimbaud; 'Translation,' by F. Scott Fitzgerald; 'Notes,' by Paul Schmidt," *Delos,* II (1968).

"WINTER DREAMS" (STORY)

K 370*
The Bedside Tales   A Gay Collection. New York: Penn, 1945.

K 371
Short Story Masterpieces, ed. Robert Penn Warren and Albert Erskine. New York: Dell, 1954.

K 372*
McLean's, 50th Anniversary Issue (15 October 1955).

K 373*
American Literature, ed. Andrew J. Porter, Henry L. Terrie, Jr., and Edward J. Gordon. Boston: Ginn, 1961, 1964.

K 374
American Literature   A College Survey, ed. Clarence A. Brown and John T. Flanagan. New York, Toronto, & London: McGraw-Hill, 1961.

K 375
American Literature: Readings and Critiques, ed. R. W. Stallman and Arthur Waldhorn. New York: Putnam, 1961.

K 376
Twelve Short Stories, ed. Marvin Magalaner and Edmond L. Volpe. New York: Macmillan, 1961.

K 377
American Literature Survey   The Twentieth Century, ed. Milton R. Stern and Seymour L. Gross. New York: Viking Press, 1962.

K 378*
The Young Writer at Work, ed. Jessie Rehder. New York: Odyssey Press, 1962.

K 379
The Modern Talent, ed. John Edward Hardy. New York: Holt, Rinehart & Winston, 1964.

K 380*
Prose and Poetry of America, Vol. III, ed. Julian L. Maline and Vernon Ruland. Syracuse: Singer, 1965.

K 381
The Short Story Classic & Contemporary, ed. R. W. Lid. New York & Philadelphia: Lippincott, 1966.

K 382
The Art of Fiction: A Handbook and Anthology, R. F. Dietrich and Roger H. Sundell. New York: Holt, Rinehart & Winston, 1967, 1974*, 1978*.

K 383
An Introduction to Literature: Fiction, ed. Theodore L. Gross and Norman Kelvin. New York: Random House, 1967.

K 384*
Fiction for Composition, ed. Bert C. Bach and Gordon Browning. Glenview, Ill.: Scott, Foresman, 1968.

K 385
American Literature Tradition & Innovation, Vol. III, ed. Harrison T. Meserole, Walter Sutton, and Brom Weber. Lexington, Mass.: Heath, 1969.

K 386*
The Jazz Age, ed. Max Bogart. New York: Scribners, 1969.

K 387
The Literature of America: Twentieth Century, ed. Mark Schorer. New York: McGraw-Hill, 1970.

K 388*
The Literature of America, Vol. II, ed. Irving Howe, Mark Schorer, and Larzer Ziff. New York: McGraw-Hill, 1971.

K 389*
Studies in the Short Story, ed. Virgil Scott. New York: Holt, Rinehart & Winston, 1971.

K 390*
The American's Search for Identity: A Reader, ed. James E. Brogan. New York: Harcourt Brace Jovanovich, 1972.

K 391*
Into America A Literary Introduction, ed. Charlotte K. Freedman and Morris Freedman. New York: Macmillan, 1972.

K 392*
Themes in American Literature, ed. Philip McFarland et al. Boston: Houghton Mifflin, 1972.

K 393*
Popular Writing in America The Interaction of Style and Audience, ed. Donald McQuade and Robert Atwan. New York: Oxford University Press, 1974.

K 394*
Modern Stories in English, ed. W. H. New and H. J. Rosengarten. New York: Crowell, 1975.

K 395*
Great American Short Stories. Pleasantville, N.Y.: The Reader's Digest Association, 1977.

K 396*
Modernism in Literature, ed. Todd K. Bender et al. New York: Holt, Rinehart & Winston, 1977.

K 397*
Fiction 100, ed. James H. Pickering. 2nd ed. New York: Macmillan, 1978.

"Absolution" was reprinted in the 1974 edition.

See K 8‡.

"THE WOMAN FROM TWENTY-ONE" (STORY)

K 398
The Girls from Esquire, ed. Frederick A. Birmingham. New York: Random House, 1952; London: Barker, 1953; London: Dragon, 1957*; London: Panther, 1961.

See B 35.

K 399
Manhattan Stories from the Heart of a Great City, ed. Seymour Krim. New York: Bantam, 1954.

"A WOMAN WITH A PAST" (STORY)

K 400
The Pleasures of the Jazz Age, ed. William Hodapp. New York: Farrar, Straus, 1948; New York: Berkley, n.d.

K 401*
Contemporary American Prose, ed. Clarence W. Wachner, Frank E. Ross, and Eva Marie Van Houten. New York: Macmillan, 1963.

K 402*
Short Stories for Discussion, ed. Albert K. Ridout and Jesse Stuart. New York: Scribners, 1965.

K 403*
The American Experience; Fiction, ed. Marjorie Wescott Barrows. New York: Macmillan, 1968.

"THE WORLD'S FAIR" (STORY)

K 404
13 Great Stories, ed. Daniel Talbot. New York: Dell, 1956.

See B 40.

"YAIS" (POEM)

K 405

The Tiger's Family Album. Princeton: Princeton University Press, 1931.

See B 15.

Appendices / Index

Appendix 1

English-Language Editions of Story Collections Published in Japan

1.13

[gothic] Contemporary English Series | [roman] [bracket] 58 [bracket] | CRAZY SUN-DAY | BY | F. SCOTT FITZGERALD | *EDITED WITH NOTES* | *BY* | K. Takamura | OSAKA KYOIKU TOSHO CO., LTD.

Tokyo & Osaka, 1972. Wrappers.

"Crazy Sunday" and "The Diamond as Big as the Ritz."

1.14

BE-173 | The Lost Generation | F. S. Fitzgerald | E. Hemingway | W. Faulkner | Edited with Notes by | Hideo Okamoto | Michio Ochi | Takaaki Niwa | BUNRI Co., Ltd.

Tokyo, 1973. Wrappers.

"Babylon Revisited."

1.15

F. SCOTT FITZGERALD | THE PAT HOBBY STORIES | Edited with Notes by | T. KO-YAMA | & | K. HOSOKOSHI | SANSYUSYA

Tokyo, 1974. Wrappers.

"Pat Hobby's Christmas Wish," "A Man in the Way," "Pat Hobby and Orson Welles," "The Homes of the Stars," and "Pat Hobby's College Days."

1.16

The Basil and Josephine Stories | [double rules] | *by F. Scott Fitzgerald* | Edited with Notes | by | HIROSHIGE YOSHIDA | & | TATSUO NAMBA | THE SIGN OF [logo] A GOOD BOOK | THE EIHÔSHA LTD. | —Tokyo—

1974. Wrappers.

"He Thinks He's Wonderful," "Forging Ahead," and "Basil and Cleopatra."

1.17

F. S. Fitzgerald | Babylon Revisited | and | Other Stories | Edited with Notes | by | FUMI ADACHI | THE HOKUSEIDO PRESS

Tokyo, 1976.

"Winter Dreams," "Absolution," and "Babylon Revisited."

1.18

F. S. Fitzgerald | *Edited with Notes* | *by* | KATSUJI TAKAMURA | [device] | Eichosha Great American Authors Series

189

Tokyo, 1977. Wrappers.

"Winter Dreams" and "The Rich Boy."

1.19

F. Scott Fitzgerald | Last Kiss | & | Other Stories | Edited with Notes | by | Takashi Tasaka | Yoshiya Chiba | SHINOZAKI [logo] SHORIN

Tokyo, 1978. Wrappers.

"Jacob's Ladder," "The Swimmers," and "Last Kiss."

Appendix 2

Unlocated Clippings

2.24
"Middle West Girl More at Home in Kitchen Than in Ballroom, Says F. Scott Fitzgerald."

Interview, 1922/1923.

Appendix 6

Movie-Writing Assignments

6.19 *(p. 325)*
Emlyn Williams's play *The Light of Heart*.

Appendix 7

Movies Made from Fitzgerald's Work

7.1 *(p. 326)*
Directed by William P. Dowlan.

Photoplay adapted by Ethel Rosemon in "The Chorus Girl's Romance," *Moving Picture Stories*, XVI (1 October 1920), 6–9.

7.2 *(p. 326)*
Scenario by Joseph F. Poland.

Note 3 (p. 327)
See Michael Adams, "Fitzgerald Filmography," *Fitzgerald/Hemingway Annual 1977*, pp. 101–109.

7.11
"The Camel's Back" (retitled *Conductor 1492*). Warner Brothers, 1924. Story by Johnny Hines; directed by Charles and Frank Hines.

See Alan Margolies, "'The Camel's Back' and *Conductor 1492*," *Fitzgerald/Hemingway Annual 1974*, pp. 87–88.

7.12
The Great Gatsby. Paramount, 1974. Screenplay by Francis Ford Coppola; directed by Jack Clayton.

7.13
The Last Tycoon. Paramount, 1976. Screenplay by Harold Pinter; directed by Elia Kazan.

Appendix 9

Contracts

Page 1 of contract for *The Last Tycoon*

194

Expenses incurred for alterations in type or plates, exceeding twenty per cent. of the cost of composition and electrotyping said work, are to be charged to the AUTHOR'S account.

The first statement shall not be rendered until six months after date of publication; and thereafter statements shall be rendered semi-annually, on the AUTHOR'S application therefor, in the months of February and August; settlements to be made in cash, four months after date of statement.

If, on the expiration of FIVE years from date of publication, or at any time thereafter, the demand for said work should not, in the opinion of said PUBLISHERS, be sufficient to render its publication profitable, then, upon written notice by said PUBLISHERS to said AUTHOR, this contract shall cease and determine; and thereupon said AUTHOR shall have the right, at **his** *option, to take from said PUBLISHERS, at cost, whatever copies of said work they may then have on hand; or, failing to take said copies at cost, then said PUBLISHERS shall have the right to dispose of the copies on hand as they may see fit, free from any percentage or royalty, and to cancel this contract.*

Provided, also, that if, at any time during the continuance of this agreement, said work shall become unsalable in the ordinary channels of trade, said PUBLISHERS shall have the right to dispose of any copies on hand paying to said AUTHOR **- fifteen (15) -** *per cent. of the net amount received therefor, in lieu of the percentage hereinbefore prescribed.*

If after two years from the date of publication the sale of said work falls below a total of five hundred (500) copies in any year, the royalty shall be TEN (10) percent for the sales that year.

In consideration of the mutuality of this contract, the aforesaid parties agree to all its provisions, and in testimony thereof affix their signatures and seals.

Witness to signature of
    John Biggs, Jr., as Executor
      of Estate of F. Scott Fitzgerald

[signature: Agnes C. Hemingway]

[signature: John Biggs, Jr.] (L. S.)
*Executor of the Estate of
F. Scott Fitzgerald*

Witness to signature of
    Charles Scribner's Sons

[signature: Charles Scribner's Sons] (L. S.)
*By Maxwell Perkins
Vice Pres.*

Page 2 of contract for *The Last Tycoon*

Appendix 10

Principal Works About Fitzgerald

Allen, Joan M. *Candles and Carnival Lights: The Catholic Sensibility of F. Scott Fitzgerald*. New York: New York University Press, 1978.

Bruccoli, Matthew J. *"The Last of the Novelists": F. Scott Fitzgerald and* The Last Tycoon. Carbondale & Edwardsville: Southern Illinois University Press, 1977.

———. *Scott and Ernest: The Authority of Failure and the Authority of Success*. New York: Random House, 1978.

Bryer, Jackson R. *F. Scott Fitzgerald: The Critical Reception*. New York: Burt Franklin, 1978.

Buttitta, Tony. *After the Good Gay Times: Asheville—Summer of '35 A Season with F. Scott Fitzgerald*. New York: Viking, 1974.

Graham, Sheilah. *The Real F. Scott Fitzgerald: Thirty-five Years Later*. New York: Grosset & Dunlap, 1976.

Smith, Scottie Fitzgerald; Matthew J. Bruccoli; and Joan P. Kerr. *The Romantic Egoists*. New York: Scribners, 1974.

Index

Pittsburgh Series in Bibliography

HART CRANE: A DESCRIPTIVE BIBLIOGRAPHY
Joseph Schwartz and Robert C. Schweik

F. SCOTT FITZGERALD: A DESCRIPTIVE BIBLIOGRAPHY
Matthew J. Bruccoli

WALLACE STEVENS: A DESCRIPTIVE BIBLIOGRAPHY
J. M. Edelstein

EUGENE O'NEILL: A DESCRIPTIVE BIBLIOGRAPHY
Jennifer McCabe Atkinson

JOHN BERRYMAN: A DESCRIPTIVE BIBLIOGRAPHY
Ernest C. Stefanik, Jr.

RING W. LARDNER: A DESCRIPTIVE BIBLIOGRAPHY
Matthew J. Bruccoli and Richard Layman

MARIANNE MOORE: A DESCRIPTIVE BIBLIOGRAPHY
Craig S. Abbott

NATHANIEL HAWTHORNE: A DESCRIPTIVE BIBLIOGRAPHY
C. E. Frazer Clark, Jr.

JOHN O'HARA: A DESCRIPTIVE BIBLIOGRAPHY
Matthew J. Bruccoli

MARGARET FULLER: A DESCRIPTIVE BIBLIOGRAPHY
Joel Myerson

RAYMOND CHANDLER: A DESCRIPTIVE BIBLIOGRAPHY
Matthew J. Bruccoli

DASHIELL HAMMETT: A DESCRIPTIVE BIBLIOGRAPHY
Richard Layman

SUPPLEMENT TO F. SCOTT FITZGERALD: A DESCRIPTIVE BIBLIOGRAPHY
Matthew J. Bruccoli

Forthcoming

JAMES GOULD COZZENS: A DESCRIPTIVE BIBLIOGRAPHY
Matthew J. Bruccoli

HENRY DAVID THOREAU: A DESCRIPTIVE BIBLIOGRAPHY
Raymond R. Borst